Wilderness Australia

Desert sunset — beyond the north Flinders Ranges, South Australia.

Storm over Kakadu, Northern Territory.

Wilderness
Australia

David McGonigal

Photography by the author, Robbi Newman and Gunter Schmida

TREASURE PRESS

David McGonigal has spent a large part of his life exploring the world's wild places. Specialising in adventure travel, his work as a writer and photographer has taken him from his home in Sydney to wilderness areas throughout Australia – from the Kimberleys in the north to South West Tasmania; the Barrier Reef and its rainforest hinterlands to the Strzelecki Track across Sturt's Stony Desert; the Blue Mountains, NSW to Kakadu, NT. He has also travelled extensively throughout the world on various assignments: trekking in Nepal, diving the Americas and the Pacific, camel riding in India, bicycling in China and hitchhiking across the roof of the world – from Tibet to Kathmandu. His stories and photographs have appeared in most major magazines and newspapers in Australia. He uses Nikon camera equipment exclusively.

Robbi Newman is one of Australia's most respected photopraphers. He has been around Australia three times on photographic assignments and has been the princpal photographer for several books. In Sydney he lives by the sea and is an avid surfer. Besides landscape and nature photography, Robbi does most of his work for the advertising industry including destination assignments for airlines. He and David McGonigal first worked together on brochures for the Australian Himalayan Expeditions – along with Ken Gilroy, the designer of this book. Robbi's travelling cameras are Leicas.

Gunter Schmida has excelled in the very specialised world of nature photography. Besides regularly providing photographs for magazines both here and in Germany, Gunter has written two books which feature his photography: "The Coldblooded Australians" and "Australian Freshwater Fishes" (with Dr John Merrick). Born in Braunschweig, West Germany, Gunter came to live in Australia in 1965.

Albino wallaby, Tasmania.

Front cover: *Victoria River, Northern Territory.*
Inside front cover: *New England Ranges, NSW.*
Back cover: *Rainforest, Lake St Clair, Tasmania.*
Inside back cover: *Billabong, Coopers Creek, South Australia.*

First published 1987 by
Reed Books Pty Ltd
3/470 Sydney Road, Balgowlah NSW 2093

This edition published in
Australia and New Zealand by
TREASURE PRESS AUSTRALIA
a division of the Octopus Publishing Group
22 Salmon Street, Port Melbourne, Victoria 3207

Text: © David McGonigal 1990

Designed by Ken Gilroy
Front and rear cover photographs by David McGonigal
Typeset by The Type Shop, Fivedock, N.S.W.
Produced by Mandarin Offset in Hong Kong

ISBN 1 86345 032 7

Coastal wildflowers, Western Australia.

Contents

Desert dune, South Australia.

Introduction

In the global dance called continental drift, Australia has been the shrinking violet leaning against the wall, watching the interplay between the others. While they collided and erupted, settled down and split asunder, Australia stayed on the sidelines providing a remarkably stable and isolated environment with unique vegetation and animals, landform and features.

Until about 200 million years ago the great majority of the world's landmasses — including Australia — formed a single gigantic whole: the supercontinent of Pangaea meaning "all lands". As the tectonic plates on which the continents lie drifted apart, North America and Eurasia moved away from the remaining continent of Gondwanaland about 135 million years ago.

By about 100 million years ago, the continental division evident today had taken place. South America and Africa had only recently split up; India had recently pared off from Australia and Antarctica in its headlong rush towards Asia, the force of that collision pushing up the highest mountains on earth — the Himalayas. Australia completed the disintegration of Gondwanaland by splitting from Antarctica, drifting northwards towards its current position.

While the grinding of African and Eurasian plates forces the European Alps to greater heights and India's inexorable push into Asia further develops the Himalayas, Australia stays remote, the smallest, driest, flattest continent on the face of the earth.

Elsewhere, civilisations rose and fell and people migrated to and fro in continuous confusing patterns. Australia remained singular in seeing the arrival of one race, the Aborigines — these first inhabitants leaving behind some of the world's oldest traces of human civilisation at Lake Mungo, western NSW. Yet this people developed such a close affinity to the land that their impact upon it was minimal. Indeed, we are only now starting to piece together what is untouched Australian wilderness and what may have been changed over 40,000 years of Aboriginal occupation.

It has been 200 years since the first permanent white settlement was established in Australia. Those two short centuries have seen more changes to the face of Australia than all the ages past. Land has been converted from forest to farming and grazing, mines have been opened and cities built. But until recently, popular opinion was that a few people in a big country could have little effect on the natural environment as a whole.

However, with the rapidly increasing momentum of modern society and its tools, Australia and indeed the world, has become too small for man

Carnarvon Gorge, Queensland.

to act with no thought for the effect of those actions on the world in which he lives. Jacques Cousteau states that there is nowhere on the ocean today where one isn't confronted by clear signs of human pollution. The seemingly endless wilderness of Australia is similarly threatened although population density remains low and many areas defy human habitation. Even in the Red Centre it is hard to find anywhere that vehicles haven't been — the days of "trackless wilderness" have passed. Spend long enough on any outback track and you are likely to see a seismic vehicle pass by — seeking mineral wealth which will, in turn, cause towns to be built and the wilderness to further recede. Wait longer and a tourist bus — albeit a four wheel drive one — will appear over the horizon as travellers push frontiers further to discover the sublime satisfaction of standing where few have stood before.

Elsewhere islands become resorts, beaches are mined or made the raw material of holiday destinations (complete with hotels and amusement grounds), mountains become ski fields, forests reduced to woodchips and the force of rivers dammed to power factories and appliances. Fortunately, as the wilderness is threatened, an enthusiasm to preserve it has arisen in the community. No longer is Progress a banner behind which any despolation can be justified. This was made clear in the successful 1983 public campaign to prevent the damming of the Franklin River in South West Tasmania. Since then, there have been other battles fought to preserve our national, natural heritage. Although not all have been won, there is a new element of accountability in any plans or transactions affecting wild Australia. It is yet to be seen if this is merely another case of

Top: Bogong high plains, Victoria.

Bottom: Waterworn rocks in a creek within the MacDonnell Ranges, Northern Territory.

Opposite: Drowned trees in Lake Argyle, Western Australia: the dam was made in the 1960's as part of the Ord River Irrigation Scheme.

"too little, too late" or whether we will pass to our children the fascinating land into which our generation were born.

The most cursory examination of the features of the Australian wilderness reveal an incredible array of natural wonders. Isolation was the reason for the evolution and continuing survival of some of the strangest creatures on earth. Few marsupials (animals whose young are born prematurely then raised within a pouch) exist elsewhere in the world yet Australia has 150 different types including koalas, wombats, possums, bandicoots, native "cats", kangaroos and wallabies. The Thylacine (or Tasmanian Tiger) was a marsupial, driven from the mainland after Aborigines brought their dingoes to the country and hunted to extinction this century. Despite a lack of family resemblance, the platypus and echidna (or spiny ant-eater) are closely related — the only two surviving families of monotremes. The platypus, a furry, egg-laying, duck-billed, web-footed mammal, was first seen by white men in 1797 but its reality was only established beyond doubt in 1802 after scientific investigation! Sharing the rivers of SE Queensland with it is the lungfish — a descendant of the first fish to put fin on land about 350 million years ago on the evolutionary path towards mankind.

Unlike the forests of the northern hemisphere, the Australian bush is a cacophony of sound. Shrieking, multicoloured parrots flash from tree to tree, currawongs warble in the dawn light and kookaburras laugh hysterically from the treetops. When black swans — the only swans found in Australia — were taken from the Swan River, WA to the governor-general of the Dutch Indies in 1697, it created great interest in Europe where "black swan" had previously been accepted as a contradiction in terms.

The landforms of Australia are similarly unique. Queensland's Great Barrier Reef, is both an endlessly complex ecosystem and the world's largest living thing. Ayers Rock, almost exactly in the centre of Australia like an enormous marker peg, is the world's largest monolith. The array of deserts and forests, beaches and islands is enormous. But the main feature of the Australian wilderness is its accessibility: every city has vast tracts of wilderness in its hinterland, easily reached within a couple of hours by road. It would take several lifetimes to fully explore Australia's wilderness but some of it is available every weekend.

Islands hold a particular fascination in the human mind so it is not unusual that Australia — the greatest island and the world's only island continent — has special appeal. Its relative isolation and late European settlement ensured that most of the world was late in discovering Australia's unique attractions. The Aborigines, first caretakers of this special and fragile environment, left much for following generations to wonder at. It remains to be seen if Australians of the future will see us as the custodians — or destroyers — of our natural heritage.

*Top: Sandstone islets off the
Port Campbell coast, Victoria*

*Opposite: Myall Lakes,
New South Wales*

The Coastline

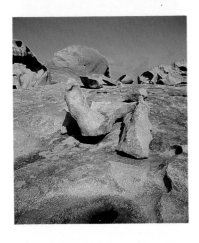

The afternoon sun was low in the sky when I drove into the small West Australian coastal town of Cervantes. A small sign pointed to a track leading to Nambung National Park and the Pinnacles. The dirt road it directed me along was terrible: as the car's suspension tied itself into spaghetti over the corrugations and ditches, the underside of the body was burnished by protruding limestone boulders. Finally, the road rose above the tunnel of shrubs and trees and into the golden glow of the setting sun.

It was like stepping out of the dark into the bright fantasy land of Oz. All around were towering sandhills dropping away to the sea a couple of kilometres away; scattered among them were the Pinnacles themselves — a vast area of pillars ranging from some the size of cars to others like tiny fingers protruding through the sand. They are moulded into fantastic shapes — some groups resemble crumbling office towers after a holocaust while others have the semblance of human forms. Spread along the coastal dunes for several kilometres, the sight challenges the perceptions while the intellect struggles to find an answer to how they came about. The larger pillars look like the ant hills of northern Australia while the small ones look like the stalagmites found in limestone caves. In fact, the similarity to stalagmites is close to the truth. The scientific explanation is that the Pinnacles are the result of coastal vegetation being engulfed by sand dunes tens of thousands of years ago. Later, rainwater dissolved sea shells then percolated this calcareous matter through the sand and redeposited it as limestone in the spaces left by the buried plants and their roots. Much more recently the dunes rolled past, leaving the tops of the limestone pillars exposed.

The Pinnacles Desert is perhaps one of the most unusual sights in a land of the bizarre. However, around the extensive shoreline of Australia there is much to fascinate the traveller. The mainland coast is 18,200 kilometres in length; when the coast of Tasmania is included it comes to just under 20,000 kilometres. Unlike the fiord-punctuated coastline of countries such as Norway, the coast of Australia is remarkably smooth — the Gulf of Carpentaria biting deep into the northern side of the continent is the most notable irregularity. From the tip of Cape York (the northernmost point of the continent at 10^0 latitude) along the Queensland coast past Rockhampton (cut by the Tropic of Capricorn) to Bundaberg at 24^0 latitude, the coast is protected by the Great Barrier Reef.

Over 2,000 kilometres long, the Great Barrier Reef is the largest coral reef in the world — the next in size lies along the coast of New Caledonia. It is made up of 2500 separate reefs. At its northern end, the Outer Reef forms a rampart at the very edge of the continental shelf. The long rolling waves of the Pacific become large breakers when suddenly confronted by the shallow waters and the reef. Further south, the reef lies well inside the edge of the continental shelf which itself slopes much more gradually at this point. Up north, the reef drops sharply to the depths of the Pacific — the 1000 fathom line is only five kilometres from its edge. Down south, the outer point of the reef lies 50 kilometres inside the 100 fathom line.

Many years ago, scientists decided to drill through the reef to see how thick the coral was above the underlying bedrock. Sites both north and south revealed about 125 metres of coral before the drills struck layers of sand and shells. Neither bore reached bedrock.

Only three of the resort islands of the Queensland coast are true coral cays made by the myriad tiny polyps that, over eons, constructed this complex masterpiece. These are Green Island off Cairns, Heron Island off Gladstone and Lady Elliot Island which lies north-east of Bundaberg. All the other resorts and most of the other islands, including the Whitsundays, are sunken mainland islands. Many of these, however, are bordered by fringing reefs so one is never far

Encroaching sand dunes on Fraser Island march forward to swallow vegetation in their path. Fraser Island in Southern Queensland is the world's largest sand island.

Opposite (from top): A pelican lumbers into the air near Port Macquarie, NSW. Although apparently clumsy and comical on land, pelicans are exquisitely graceful in flight and glide better than any other bird.

Estuary plant growing in a pool within Kakadu National Park, Northern Territory.

Remarkable Rocks, Kangaroo Island, SA.

Seaweed deposited by a falling tide on a waveworn rock on the isolated south west coast of Tasmania.

from an exquisite underwater world. Throughout these and the other reefs which comprise the Great Barrier Reef live over 30,000 different animal species — including over 4000 types of shell fish and 2000 species of fish. The rich colours adopted by many in the neverending battle to breed and escape predators provides a sight without parallel for anyone who dons a mask and flippers — or takes the less adventurous vantage point of a glass-bottomed boat.

The Great Barrier Reef Marine Park has been proclaimed in various stages since 1938. It now includes 98 percent of the Great Barrier Reef itself and is in the World Heritage Listing — the inventory of the world's unique and precious places. Preserving the Reef within a well regulated National Park and affording it the protection of World Heritage Listing are both important steps in ensuring the reef's survival.

Around Brisbane lie two of the world's great sand islands: Fraser Island, the world's largest and Moreton Island which has the largest sand dunes in the world. While Moreton Island is considerably smaller than Fraser Island (17,000 hectares compared with Fraser Island's 160,000) it has Mount Tempest (283 metres) the highest permanent sand hill in the world. Fraser Island was presumed to be a promontory and named Sandy Cape by Captain Cook in 1770. It was subsequently discovered to be an island and was renamed in honour of Captain James Fraser who arrived on the island in 1836 after being shipwrecked — he and many of his party were subsequently slain by the aboriginal inhabitants of the island.

Fraser Island is 125 kilometres long, from 5 to 22 kilometres wide and its sand hills rise to almost 250 metres. The largest freshwater lake on the island is 60 metres deep and there are lush rainforests in the interior. Not all the island is sand: along the eastern shore there is an outcrop of volcanic rock which probably

provided the anchor to retain the sands which form the bulk of the island. Fraser Island is home to over 200 birds as well as numerous marsupials, reptiles and even a herd of wild brumbies. Only in 1976 was a ban placed on the export of sand from Fraser Island. Unfortunately, regeneration after mining is likely to be slow as many of the NSW rivers which swept sand into the ocean to be carried to Fraser Island are now dammed and their sand producing qualities greatly impeded.

There is a distinct difference between the coastal formations of NSW and Queensland. While the Queensland coast is littered with islands and protected by the Reef, along the NSW shores the coast becomes steeper and the continental shelf much narrower. Scenically, it is one of the most attractive parts of the whole Australian coastline — lush, rolling green hills give way to towering headlands and many wide empty beaches.

Although much of Sydney's foreshore is crowded by houses, flats and offices, fortunately, the original coastal formation can't be obscured. Several harbour and oceanside reserves ensure that it is still possible to appreciate the natural beauty of the setting. Since Governor Arthur Phillip sailed into Sydney Harbour (or, more correctly, Port Jackson) on January 21, 1788 and described it as "the finest harbour in the world", there have been few who disagree with that judgement. Sydney Harbour is a drowned valley and, as it has no major rivers flowing into it, free of silting. Below the hills and cliffs of the harbour are many sandy beaches and the oceanside suburbs have the standard NSW coastal configuration of one headland and golden beach after the other.

When the Royal National Park, south of the city was proclaimed in April 1879, Australia became the second country in the world to declare a National

Opposite page: The prosaic title of "tessellated" or mosaic pavement obscures one of the most unusual features of Tasmania. Lying below a cliff face en route to the convict ruins of Port Arthur, the pavement consists of innumerable blocks of vertically joined sandstone which have been worn by waves. The end result seems too regular to be a natural formation but rather quarry tiling wrought by a giant hand.

Above: It is fitting that these trees tower over the ruins of the shipyards of the Sarah Island convict settlement in the middle of Macquarie Harbour on Tasmania's rugged west coast. Now the area is part of the Wild Rivers National Park and tall trees stand sentinel over the ruins of the loggers' and carpenters' settlement.

Opposite page: Patterns in sand, Great Australian Bight, South Australia.

Above: coastal sandstone, readily worn into fantastic shapes, is nature's modelling clay — this NSW rock pool mirrors the clouds of the late afternoon sky.

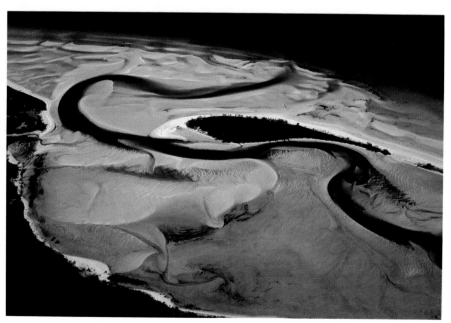

Fraser Island, Queensland - the sand of which it's composed comes from beaches as far away as Sydney. Considering its wave-borne sandy origin, the island is remarkably fertile and this is reflected in the brown streams, stained by decaying vegetable matter, flowing to the coast.

Above: pelicans overflying the Coorong, South Australia.

Right: It is unfortunate for crayfish that they are regarded as a delicacy around the world and thereby sowing the seeds of their own destruction. They are found — and caught — around Australia.

Opposite page:
Top: the massive force of waves in shaping continents is inestimable. This photograph was taken in northern NSW where waves sweep unimpeded out of the vastness of the Pacific Ocean. Much of the east coast of the Australian mainland north of the NSW border is protected by the Great Barrier Reef.

Bottom: Cormorants sometimes fish by diving from perches by the streamside.

Park. (The first was Yellowstone in the USA.) In many ways, the history of the Royal National Park parallels the growing realisation of the need to preserve the environment. These days, we think of a National Park as a part of our natural heritage set aside to be enjoyed and appreciated in perpetuity. Sydney's "National Park" (the "Royal" was added in 1955 after it was visited by Queen Elizabeth II) wasn't initially intended to fulfil that role at all. Rather, it was to be developed as Sydney's "pleasure garden" modelled more on Hampstead Heath in London than the Australian bush: forests were cut down to make way for lawns, ornamental gardens and imported species of trees. Deer were introduced in 1885 and, until 1922, Park Trusts were selling licences for logging within the Park. In the Second World War the Park was used for army training exercises. By 1967 when the NSW National Parks and Wildlife Service was established, the Park was a mess. However, since then steps have been taken to return it to its natural state — with considerable success. There are still deer in the Park but, apart from such non-Australian aberrations, it is now back to being an area of attractive Australian scenery.

After Cape Howe, on the border of NSW and Victoria, the mainland coastline turns towards the west. Bass Strait which divides Tasmania and the mainland is very shallow with an average width of 210 kilometres. The strait is well named after the naval surgeon and noted explorer George Bass (1771-1803) who both developed the theory that Van Diemen's Land (now Tasmania) was an island then circumnavigated it with Mathew Flinders to prove his hypothesis. Bass disappeared on a voyage to South America in 1803.

Tasmania is a heart-shaped island about one third the size of the State of Victoria. At its widest points, the island is about 300 kilometres in both length and breadth. It's a mountainous place — particularly in the central highlands and

The coastline of Sydney and much of NSW consists of one headland after another (above), linked by crescent shaped golden sand beaches (below).

Opposite page: Water lilies in Kakadu National Park wetlands, Northern Territory.

Top left: reed banks alongside the Hawkesbury River, NSW

Top right: sunset over the Hawkesbury.

Bottom left: water worn sandstone rocks in Sydney Harbour.

Bottom right: formation paddling by ducks on a waterway near Sydney.

Opposite page: Banded Stilt (Cladorhynchus leucephalus), Western Australia.

along the rugged west coast. In many ways, it's in direct contrast to the bulk of Australia- a small and verdant green gem alongside the "wide brown land". Travelling through much of Australia is a battle against vast distances with little in between: in Tasmania, a hard day's travelling may only cover a few kilometres of dense forest. Whereas the major difficulty for early explorers elsewhere in Australia was thirst and a perennial shortage of water, in Tasmania the problem is often too much water encouraging the growth of impenetrable rainforest and turning tracks into quagmires.

Still, Tasmania is very much typically Australia in providing large tracts of land which have been relatively little disturbed by people. This is particularly true of the remote south west corner of the island, an area often lashed by the westerly gales of the Roaring Forties and with a very high annual rainfall — up to 3500 millimetres in some places. Unfortunately, Tasmanian governments have traditionally seen this mountainous wilderness as the raw material of hydro-electric power and wood chips — not as a showplace of a unique environment. As public understanding of the need to conserve wilderness has outstripped government awareness of this shift in opinion, there has been conflict. First came Lake Pedder, one of Australia's earliest major conservation battles. Pedder was a highland lake with a spectacularly beautiful white quartzite beach. Despite an intensive fight by those who thought that the area — part of a National Park — should be conserved, Lake Pedder disappeared under the rising waters of a hydro-electric dam in 1972.

Although Lake Pedder was lost, those with an interest in the wilderness could console themselves in the bush remaining. Undoubtably, the jewel in the crown of

Tasmania's wilderness is the Franklin River, one of the world's few truly wild rivers. The Franklin is an essential part of the Tasmanian Wilderness National Parks which, like the Great Barrier Reef, is on the World Heritage List. Flowing for about 120 kilometres through the heart of the western ranges, rafters and kayakers find the river to be a sublime mixture of heart-stopping action in rapids interspersed with tranquil reaches past otherwise inaccessible riverside scenery which is some of the most hauntingly beautiful in the world.

Possibly because the Franklin river is so pristine, so seemingly inviolate, that the decision by the Tasmanian government to allow the lower Gordon to be dammed flooding back up the Franklin was greeted with such dismay and such widespread opposition. The Tasmanian government, led by Robin Gray, remained intransigent. However, the Federal Labor Party, campaigning on a promise to intervene to stop the dam, was elected before work on the dam had gone very far. Once in power, the newly-elected Federal Government passed legislation to prevent the dam and that legislation was subsequently upheld by the High Court. The Franklin River was saved.

One the other side of Tasmania — the populous east coast which, although only a couple of hundred kilometres away, is a world away from the southwest wilderness — lies the Tasman Peninsula, a small promontory with several fascinating features. The Tasman Peninsula is the most popular tourist destination in Tasmania largely because it is here that the ruins of the Port Arthur penal colony are found. The earlier penal establishment at Macquarie Harbour had proven too difficult to service so Lieutenant-Governor Colonel George Arthur looked elsewhere. Port Arthur provided the ideal location for a maximum security prison. It was easily reached by ship from Hobart yet remained virtually impossible to escape by water. By land, Port Arthur is reached via two very

narrow isthmuses — East Bay Neck and Eaglehawk Neck — both of which are easy to guard effectively. The penal institution started operating in 1830 and closed in 1877 — 24 years after the end of transportation to Tasmania. Fittingly, for so brutal a place, the church built in the grounds was never named and never consecrated — today only the walls remain standing.

Near Eaglehawk Neck are the Tessellated Pavement, Tasmans Arch, the Blowhole and Devils Kitchen. The Tessellated Pavement is a flat expanse of rock at the water's edge which has been fractured into a series of small rectangular blocks; the other three attractions are various stages of the undermining effect of ocean waves. The Blowhole has been created by waves hollowing out along a fault line – in big seas,waves pound into this fracture and are thrown many metres into the air. Tasmans Arch and the Devils Kitchen were tunnels, too, before the inside roofs collapsed leaving the arch of one and the deep, narrow ravine of the other.

Across Bass Strait and about 250 kilometres southwest of Melbourne is Port Campbell National Park. It is reached via the Great Ocean Road which begins at Torquay near Geelong and finishes at Peterborough — 300 kilometres of spectacular coastal scenery. The Great Ocean Road was built to honour the servicemen of the First World War and was finished in 1932. For much of its length, the Otway Ranges form a fitting inland backdrop to what is probably Australia's best known coastal drive - the road cuts through the forests of the ranges at Apollo Bay. However, the most compelling sights along the road are at Port Campbell. Here the coast is a raised limestone plain dropping in vertical cliffs to the surf below. The soft limestone has worn rapidly and it is this erosion which provides the most notable sights of the National Park. For the eddies and ebbs haven't worn the coastline evenly — in many cases they have cut behind some blocks leaving them as off-shore islets. The best known of the many stacks

Top: pelican in flight, Myall Lakes, NSW.

Bottom: A NSW beach.

Opposite page: the still waters of Myall Lakes, NSW are in strong contrast to the pounding breakers of the ocean only a short distance away across a band of sand dunes. Myall Lakes lie in a shallow basin bounded by the sand dunes and low inland hills.

Above: a seagull soars over Barrenjoey Headland north of Sydney.

Opposite page (top): Sunrise highlights a thin band of land between ocean and river in northern NSW. (bottom) the stark yellow of a coastal sand dune highlights the cumulus cloud formed by thermal currents on a hot summer day.

and pillars along the coast are the Twelve Apostles, a group of varying sized stacks standing sentinel near the shore. Showing the tenacity of plants, many wear caps of growing heath while others have been left bald by the salt-laden on-shore winds.

The Murray, Australia's greatest river — 2600 kilometres long and draining an area of over 100 million hectares — doesn't flow directly into the sea. Instead it flows into Lake Alexandrina, South Australia, which opens to the sea in an convoluted fashion past numerous islands and sand bars. The final exit of the waters of the Murray is a tiny gap at the northern end of the Coorong, the long saltwater lagoon bounded by sand dunes which separates the Southern Ocean from the south east coast of SA. The name "Coorong", which is the corruption of an Aboriginal word meaning "neck", is used to describe the lagoon and the surrounding country. Younghusband Peninsula, a narrow strip of sandhills only one to three kilometres wide, divides the lagoon from the sea. The area was first sighted by Europeans in 1837 — in the 1850's Victorian gold-rush it was the main route from Adelaide to the diggings and the track was lined with shanties and hotels.

East of the Murray mouth is the beginning of the dry part of the continent. All along the east coast of the mainland and the whole of Tasmania, there are rivers draining the inland areas. It is fitting that the Murray, the biggest, marks the boundary between the arid and humid zones. Much of the rest of the continent drains inward, to evaporate from the salt lakes of central and western Australia.

The most conspicuous features of South Australia west of Adelaide are Kangaroo Island and Spencer Gulf and Gulf St. Vincent separated by the Yorke Peninsula. Kangaroo Island was the first place in South Australia to be settled — by sealers and whalers from 1803 on: "respectable settlement" began in 1836 at what is now Adelaide. The north of the island is quite gentle — particularly by comparison with the rugged limestone crags of the south west. There are colonies of sea lions, penguins and fur seals on the island. Both gulfs terminate in salt marshes and mangroves which are too far south to harbour a wide variety of

Looking across Tasmania's Macquarie Harbour towards Mount Sorell and the West Coast Range, mountains seemingly rise in tiers to the horizon. If wilderness is an absence of civilisation, the island in the foreground certainly qualifies: it lies near the infamous convict settlement of Sarah Island and was used as solitary confinement for recalcitrant prisoners. The settlement was abandoned in 1833.

Top: Remarkable Cave on the Tasman Peninsula is unusual in having two entrances from the sea with each channel combining into a large cavern which is accessible at low tide. From a certain position (and with a healthy imagination) it's claimed that one of the entrances appears as a map of Tasmania. However, most visitors who venture into the cave find the most overwhelming thought is of human frailty — with tonnes of rock overhead and the surf crashing against the entrance, sending shallow waves across the sandy floor to the visitors' feet.

Top: The rounded solid granite shapes of The Hazards of the Freycinet Peninsula are clearly visible across Coles Bay on Tasmania's east coast. Although they are now part of a National Park, in early days they provided the facia of several Hobart Buildings.

Bottom: The beach at Ulverstone on the north coast of Tasmania looks straight across Bass Strait. From here, cloud formations at the front of air masses, which become scrambled by topography over the mainland, can be seen as sweeping bands across the sky.

A breeding colony of crested terns (Sterna bergii) in Victoria.

Wilson's Promontory, Victoria, is the southernmost point of the Australian mainland. Originally part of the land bridge joining Tasmania and the mainland, it became an island when the sea level rose. About 10,000 years ago — yesterday in geological terms — the sand bar was formed which made Wilson's Promontory part of the mainland again.

Some of the most spectacular coastal scenery in Australia is to be seen along Victoria's Great Ocean Road (above). Perhaps the most famous features are the Twelve Apostles within the Port Campbell National Park. These large sandstone islets have been formed by waves eating away the raised coastline — eventually, they too will succumb to wave erosion and disappear entirely.

mangrove species.

Travelling west from the Eyre Peninsula, the highway borders the Great Australian Bight. The beginning of the bight is where the continental shelf widens greatly. From here until Esperance in Western Australia the Nullarbor Plain, a remarkably flat, raised limestone tableland falls sheer to the water's edge. At the end of the bight, the continental shelf narrows again and the coastline becomes less uniform and is broken by the numerous islands of the Archipelago of the Recherche.

Unlike the east coast which has been formed by a series of uplifts and periods of volcanic activity, the south coast of Australia still closely matches the configuration of the side of Antarctica that Australia broke away from when the continents drifted apart. Even so, there are only a few sections of the coast where the layers of old bedrock extend right to the shore. They do in the coastal section between Albany and Esperance. Here the western granite shield meets the Southern Ocean in a series of rugged headlands and tiny islets. After the coastal forests of giant karri, tingle and jarrah, the coast curves to the northwest and Cape Leeuwin before cutting due north.

Rottnest Island off the coast at Freemantle is a remnant of an ancient limestone shore now largely drowned. Its unfortunate name — the Dutch word for "Rat's nest" was given by the Dutch mariner Willem de Vlamingh in 1696. He named it after the small grey animals he saw on the island — rather than rats, the creatures he saw were quokkas, a species of small wallaby. Northwards, past

The Coorong, south of Adelaide, is a remarkable stretch of water separated from the Great Australian Bight by a thin strip of land, the Younghusband Peninsula. Coorong is derived from an aboriginal word meaning a "narrow neck of water". The Peninsula consists of rolling sand dunes covered by low vegetation.

the Pinnacles Desert, the shore is smooth and unbroken but there are several off-shore reefs most notably Houtman Abrolhos. This reef is further south than almost any in the world and its existence is a clear indication of the exceptionally warm ocean currents near the West Australian coast. Many of the other reefs along the west coast are not coral reefs but rather sandstone reefs formed after coastal dunes hardened into rocks and were then drowned by rising sea levels. The sea level has only been as it is at present for about 6000 years.

These "dune rock" reefs form an almost continuous line for three hundred kilometres south of North West Cape and about five kilometres offshore. Large breakers rolling in from the Indian Ocean dissipate their energy against the reefs so the coastal beaches are well protected almost as if within a lagoon.

After North West Cape, the coastline is protected not only by off-shore reefs but also a widening of the continental shelf. There are few sea cliffs or headlands — the predominant scenery is wide beach fronts and large tidal plains with some mangroves. The ocean is warm enough here to encourage the growth of coral reefs and these are interspersed with large calcareous algal platforms built on dune reefs. Just as the dune reefs around North West Cape are prime examples of their kind so too are these algal reefs.

Wilderness Australia

On the southernmost point of Kangaroo Island which lies a short distance off the South Australian shore are some of Australia's best natural sculptures. Admiral's Arch (opposite) is the product of the combined effects of sea water and rain water: the huge limestone arch, sitting on a granite base, was formed by the pounding seas hollowing out the limestone. To this has been added an overhanging fringe of stalactites resembling a tassled curtain over the immensity of the arch. These are the result of rain water percolating through the limestone arch then forming deposits where it drips from the roof into the ocean below.

Nearby, Remarkable Rocks (above) are a series of granite boulders, worn by the elements into fantastic shapes.

Although the Coorong (opposite) is paralleled by the Princes Highway for part of its length and is less than 200 kilometres from Adelaide by road (about 70 km as the crow flies), standing on its shores one can feel as if there is no-one else on earth.

In times of drought, the waterways of the Coorong are a refuge for numerous birds — as well as the pelicans for which the area is noted.

Above, bottom: Near Albany, Western Australia, the division between land and sea is blurred with numerous islands and rocks extending from the shores into the waters of the Southern Ocean.

Top: From the air, Geikie Gorge in the rugged Kimberleys of northern Western Australia looks like a gash through a coral reef after someone pulled the plug on the ocean. This isn't far from the truth — the Geikie range was part of a fringing reef back in the Devonian age (known as "the age of fishes") and remains one of the world's best preserved fossil coral reefs. Since changes in ocean levels left the range high and dry, the Fitzroy River has cut through the range on its way to the coast. Besides a large population of freshwater crocodiles, the gorge also contains sawfish and stingrays — fish normally found in the ocean — whose ancestors migrated more than 300 kilometres inland to found the colonies at Geikie.

Bottom: The black swan (Cygnus antratus) is an emblem of Western Australia and is found throughout the southern parts of the State and elsewhere in southern Australia.

The Kimberley coast in the north of the State is a magnificent area where deep flooded ravines are navigable for many kilometres and several archipelagos fringe the coast. Like Albany in the south, ancient bedrock comes right to the shore in high, steep cliffs. It's an area with tremendous tides — up to twelve metres in places. There are numerous coral platform reefs off-shore. Unlike the coast right back around to the mouth of the Murray in South Australia, the Kimberleys is the start of relatively moist conditions again — at least during the monsoonal wet season. The north coast, which starts here and continues around to the top of Cape York, has about half Australia's major rivers and they carry a disproportionately high level of sediment to the sea because they flow fast and furious in the few months of the year when they are in flood. The Ord River of the Kimberleys has been recorded as carrying 250 tonnes of mud per second. The end result of the resultant deposition are estuarine clay pans, a favoured habitat of the estuarine or saltwater crocodile.

During the dry season these tidal plains may only be flooded by the occasional extra-large tide but in the wet season the mangroves may be well seawards of the backflooded shoreline. This may occur throughout the Top End but is particularly common in the Gulf of Carpentaria. The mangroves can even survive the big seas which sometimes arise.

In geological terms it was not too long ago that much of what is now land was underwater — the whole of the Canning Basin south of Derby was part of a tropical sea during the Devonian Period 350 million years ago. A vast coral reef fringed what is now the mainland north of Derby then cut back in near Kununurra before extending up the northern coast. This reef is clearly exposed near Kununurra and bordering the King Leopold Ranges close to Fitzroy Crossing, a tiny remote settlement in the heart of the Kimberleys. Geikie and

Windjana gorges and Tunnel Creek are all part of this reef and the area is rich in marine fossils which show that back 350 million years ago, corals were less important in constructing the reef than another now extinct group of organism called stromatopoids.

Bordering Geikie Gorge National Park is Fossil Downs which, at just over a million acres is one of the country's largest cattle stations and the only one of the Kimberley giants still in the hands of the original founding family — the MacDonalds. It was settled at the conclusion of the longest cattle drive the world has ever seen — the three MacDonald brothers left Goulburn, NSW in the mid 1880's and took several years to reach their eventual home deep in the Kimberleys. Fossil Downs takes its name from the marine fossils found on the site — beside the main range, there are several atoll-type reefs within the wide boundaries of Fossil Downs.

Darwin lies on a squarish peninsula between Joseph Bonaparte Gulf east of Kimberley and the Gulf of Carpentaria. Only a few hours drive to the east of Darwin is Kakadu National Park with the new, and recently accessible, Gurig National Park on Cobourg Peninsula to its north and the large Aboriginal Reserve of Arnhem Land to the east. Arnhem Land is not generally accessible to visitors but shares many of the same features as Kakadu.

Kakadu is one of the most spectacular National Parks in Australia and a highlight of any visit to the Top End. It comprises the blacksoil floodplains of the South Alligator and East Alligator rivers and the Arnhem Escarpment. Besides fishing for the barramundi that are plentiful within the park, there are three main reasons to visit Kakadu: the scenery, wildlife and Aboriginal rock paintings. During the wet summer season, moving around the park is difficult as the floodplains (as the name suggests) are largely under water. However, when the

Opposite: In the unfrequented northwest of the continent, Victoria River is little known but reflects Australia at its best. Lieutenant Stokes who discovered the valley in 1839 wrote: "Here the river makes a wide sweep southwards and the hills close in to form a spectacular gorge". Victoria River settlement and this valley are in the Northern Territory, 195 kilometres from Katherine on the way to Kununurra.

Above, top: A female boofhead tortoise (Emyduna australis) found around the Victoria River and Kimberley region.

Middle: The archer fish has an unusual hunting method — it squirts water out of its mouth with remarkable accuracy, knocking insects from branches above the river then catching them as they fall.

Bottom: The harmless Johnstone River crocodile (Crocodylus johnstonii) is found in rivers throughout northern Australia. However, it shares many of its habitats with its less innocuous cousin: the ferocious saltwater crocodile (Crocodylus porosus).

Opposite: Cobourg Peninsula on the northernmost tip of the Northern Territory is a microcosm of tropical landscapes: sandy beaches covered in shells, coral reefs, high coastal headlands and mangrove-lined shores, tidal channels and rivers. In Victoria, Australia has mangrove stands further from the equator than at any other point in the world. Up in the tropics, well suited to mangroves, they proliferate if left undisturbed and up to 30 different species may combine to form a low closed forest. They are important as habitats for many creatures and the breeding grounds for fish.

Left (from the top): Only a short distance upstream from where the Victoria River flows as a major river, it becomes a series of pools with the river flowing beneath the sand between them.

A Great Egret (Egretta alba) hunts for aquatic animals in the shallows of a pool.

The receding tide has decoratively draped seaweed on shells which cover a beach on the Cobourg Peninsula. The variety and quality of shells in this area adds to the attractions of the area and, as it lies within Gurig National Park, regulations ensure that the shells aren't removed by visitors.

Opposite: Baby freshwater crocodiles hatch out of the egg towards the end of the year — there are between three and 25 eggs laid by each adult female. The nests are normally in sandy banks which the female will excavate at the time of hatching to help the hatchling to emerge. It is fortunate that crocodile can live for up to 100 years because less than 5% of hatchlings survive to reach adulthood.

Top: Crocodiles are cold blooded and, in cool weather, must spend hours basking in the sun. Eating all night and sunbaking all day may seem like an easy life but it obviously does terrible things to their skin! These two saltwater crocodiles show their cavenous mouths and impressive display of teeth.

Middle: Unlike the timid freshwater crocodile, saltwater crocodiles can be aggressive and, on occasion, have attacked — and killed — humans venturing into their domain. They are Australia's most feared native inhabitants although, fortunately, attacks on humans are still rare. However, we remain more of a threat to them than vice versa.

rains stop and the waters dry up and retreat to ever-decreasing lagoons and billabongs, the wildlife of the park is forced to seek them out. Magpie geese, spoonbills, pelicans, jabirus and sea eagles are all common sights on a boat trip around Yellow Waters billabong- it's estimated that Kakadu is home to one third of Australia's bird species. Not all Kakadu's inhabitants are so attractive however: saltwater crocodiles can been seen sunning themselves on riverbanks throughout the park — along with their timid and harmless cousins, the Johnstone River (or freshwater) crocodile.

The Kakadu National Park is immense: 1 300 000 hectares (with more extensions planned) but it is richness of the park in so many ways that warrants its inclusion on the list of World Heritage sites — one of the first Australian sites to be granted this honour. Besides extensive birdlife Kakadu has over 50 different mammals, 1000 plant species, numerous amphibians and reptiles and innumerable insects.

Kakadu has been Aboriginal land for over 30,000 years. Some of the cave paintings within the park are 18,000 years old — contemporaries of the palaeolithic cave paintings found in France. The area is rich in Aboriginal folklore from over 20,000 years of continual habitation yet it was only in 1978 that Aboriginal claims to the Kakadu area were accepted. By 1979, the owners had leased Kakadu back to the Australian National Parks and Wildlife Service making

Opposite: The Arhemland Escarpment drops sheer to the floodplains below. Twin Falls is one of the most beautiful areas of Kakadu National Park with the cascading stream dropping into a tranquil pool below.

Top: Seasonal variations are great in the Top End — in the wet season, most of the Kakadu plains are covered by water, access is difficult and wildlife scattered. However, towards the end of the dry months, waterways have shrunk to series of small billabongs — animals and birds are forced into greater concentration around them.

Bottom: Midway between Darwin and Kakadu lies a battlefield between man and nature — with a clear victory to nature. An attempt to start a rice plantation near what is now Fogg Dam failed when flocks of birds devoured the crops. Even today, the Sacred Ibis (Threskiornis aethiopica) pictured here is just one of the many types of birds found in abundance here — perhaps waiting for dessert.

it accessible to everyone. However, controversy still hangs heavy over the park — within its confines is Ranger uranium mine at Jabiru and other uranium deposits have been found inside the boundaries of Kakadu.

Those visitors who take the time to visit Jabiru find it to be an incongruous suburban development at great contrast to the raw beauty of the surrounding countryside. It's only a few hours drive from the manicured lawns and supermarket of Jabiru to two of the most wonderful places in Australia: Twin Falls and the neighbouring Jim Jim Falls. The falls at Jim Jim can be reached by a short walk along a narrow defile. At the end of the canyon, it widens out to an amphitheatre filled with a large, clear, tranquil pool. Most visitors come in winter when the fall is a mere trickle — a goal to swim for and take a soapless shower standing on the rock ledge below. In The Wet, the falls become a roaring torrent pouring off the escarpment; the plunge pool a maelstrom barely seen through water spray. Unfortunately, at this time the falls are only accessible by aircraft so few witness the full majesty of Jim Jim.

Twin Falls requires more effort to reach in the dry season but the endeavour is well rewarded. After swimming a few hundred metres along a peaceful stream hemmed in by high rock walls one emerges into a wide basin where the veil-like falls stream down onto the side of a beautiful palm-shaded beach. The area of Twin Falls is one of the most serene natural settings imaginable and an oft-

recalled memory that remains clear to everyone who has sought out this special place in the wonderland that is Kakadu.

Cobourg Peninsula a short flight to the north of Kakadu — over the mudflats and tidal floodplains of the East Alligator River is deeply divided by Port Essington, a large harbour which was the scene of one of the first — and most disastrous — attempts to settle the north of Australia. Mismanagement and poor communications ensured that from the time the settlement was established in 1838, it was doomed to failure — it was abandoned in 1849. Visitors arriving now to cruise and fish the blue waters of Cobourg look to the shell-strewn beaches and well wooded headlands and it looks idyllic. However, for the British troops battling an unfamiliar climate, sickness and irregular supplies must have viewed it with distaste: the dismal ruins of Victoria Settlement, Port Essington are still clearly evident but the forest is doing its best to obscure the remains.

The numerous beaches of Cobourg are among the least frequented in Australia. They fringe no large towns or cities and have not been exploited for mineral wealth. In both usage and location they are as far removed as can be from the crowded beaches of south eastern Australia. The stretch of coast between Fraser Island and the Victorian/South Australian border — taking in Tasmania — has over half the total population of Australia living near its shores. One of the major advantages of living in an uncrowded land is that it remains possible to find a deserted beach which would be lined with houses and shops — or hotels and apartments — almost anywhere else in the world. There is something elemental and satisfying in leaving the only footsteps in the sand — perhaps that's why Daniel Defoe's *Robinson Crusoe* touched a universal chord.

However, uncluttered beaches are increasing difficult to find — particularly among the crowded east coast. Wilderness is losing out to the quest for waterfront

Top (from left): Buffalo were introduced into Australia from Indonesia last century and can be found throughout the top of the Northern Territory. They now constitute a major environmental problem. In the words of one ranger "Buffaloes are the single most destructive force in Kakadu and unless we succeed in eradicating them, they threaten to destroy much of the floodplains with their wallows and hoof gouges."

A Kakadu wetland swamp.

A Jabiru or black necked stork (Xenorhynchus asiaticus).

A Great egret (Egretta alba)

Opposite, bottom: The East Alligator River in Arhemland has some of the most spectacular scenery in the region but access is restricted under the terms of Aboriginal Lands.

Opposite: A green tree python (Chondropython viridis), Cape York, Queensland.

Top, middle and bottom: The Great Barrier Reef is the world's largest living thing, the most extensive coral reef system in the world and Australia's greatest natural wonder. The outer reef lies over 300 kilometres from the Queensland shore at the discontinuous southern end but further north becomes almost a single solid wall which, in places, is only 12 kilometres from the coast. Within this sheltering boundary, the sea floor rarely reaches a depth of 30 metres and throughout its length, islands and reefs protrude above the surface. Early explorers had great difficulty in picking a path through the reef and, even today, many ships still end their days aground on its coral shoals. From the air, the deep channel at the edge of Hardy Reef, east of Hayman Island, is very clearly defined but the path is not so clear from water level. Each platform reef such as Hardy may have one or more lagoons within — all with a seemingly random abundance of coral.

Top: Lady Elliot Island at the southernmost end of the Reef is a typical coral cay — although larger than many and with a permanent resort, it still rises only a few metres above the surrounding sea.

Middle: A Pandanus seed lying on a rocky beach.

blocks and "ocean views". Urban sprawl has not just cut into the coastal wilderness, it has changed it irretrievably. The clearing of vegetation has set the sand dunes of Kurnell in Sydney loose again — the beach ridges are being consumed by moving dunes. The construction of dams and weirs on NSW rivers means that the area damaged by the sand mining of Fraser Island may never regenerate as there is less sand reaching the sea. Sandmining near Myall Lake, NSW has destroyed the blackbutt and angophora forests which grew there — large trees which rarely grow in a pure sand environment such as this. The recent road pushed through Daintree rainforest has proved even more disastrous than many people predicted — not only was the forest itself carved open, the erosion run-off in the wet season is harming the surrounding coastal waters. Attempts to artificially create and preserve a coastal environment appear doomed to failure as the resort beaches of the Gold Coast are swept away by longshore ocean currents.

It is hard to rate levels of destruction — any loss of irreplaceable natural environment is tragic. However, the clearing of mangrove swamps along the east coast to make way for housing development, resorts and marinas may have economic as well as environmental consequences. For the tangled roots of the trees of mangrove swamps are important breeding grounds for many fish and crustaceans such as prawns. Attacked on both fronts: over-fished and deprived of essential breeding grounds, the long term consequences for Australia's fish population is uncertain.

As population patterns clearly show, Australians cling to the edge of the continent, looking to the coast rather than the vast inland as the place to live and the most desirable holiday destination. That makes the coastal wildernesses the ones most under threat from development and the ones most essential to conserve. It's not merely the needs of all Australians being more important than

the privileges of a few, it is essential that we preserve the nation's untrammelled, wonderful coastline.

Top: the Silver Gull or Sea Gull (Larus Novaehollandiae) is universal and ubiquitous along the nation's shores — it's also found in New Caledonia and New Zealand.

Middle: the Rainbow Bee-eater spends summer anywhere on mainland Australia but in winter prefers the warmth of islands north of the continent.

Above: Rainbow Bay in Cooloola National Park, west of Gympie Queensland, is a popular tourist destination.

Right (from top): Double Island Point, Rainbow Beach is only accessible by a four-wheel-drive track along the beach.

Middle: Captain Cook found the passage between the mainland and these islands on Whitsunday 1770 and named both the passage and the largest island in the group after the day of discovery.

Bottom: Fraser Island is the world's largest sand island.

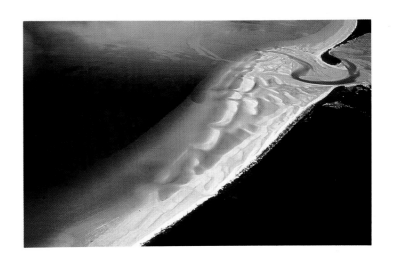

Forests

We had only walked a few hundred metres from Cradle Mountain Lodge when the path we were on left the open grasslands and plunged into a dense temperate rainforest. Walking down from bright sunlight into the muted lighting of the rainforest was like stepping into a cathedral, its roof a canopy of dark green leaves supported by the pillars of the tall trees and lit by shafts of light filtering through the branches onto the ground below. The forest floor was a rich green carpet of moss and grass with contrasting dense mats of fallen leaves. The pews of this natural hall were old, fallen trees now ornately decorated by multi-coloured lichens and mosses; the font — the shimmering waters of the river flowing gently over the rocky stream bed.

Further along the trail there were breaks in the forest providing views of nearby hills. Watching the birds flitter through the trees as a wallaby passed nearby and an eagle soared above, it was a peaceful place where not a sound of human habitation could be heard.

Australia's forests are predominantly around the fringes of the continent. They run in a continual band east of the Kimberleys, Western Australia through the Northern Territory then extend deeper inland in Queensland before narrowing again in NSW, covering a lot of Victoria then petering out around the Victoria-South Australia border. Tasmania is heavily forested. Scrub and desert extend from inland areas directly onto the coast for all of South Australia and most of Western Australia as far north as the Kimberleys. The only exception to this is in the southwest corner of Western Australia which contains an isolated forest area which, oddly enough, has some of the largest trees in Australia — over 4000 of the 6000 plants here aren't found anywhere else. Woodlands, which are broadly defined as areas where the distance between trees is greater than the height of the

Previous pages, top: Enchanted Forest, Lake St Clair, Tasmania.

Right: The camouflage pattern of a Snow gum in the Snowy Mountains of NSW is one of the more distinctive ways the Australian snowfields differ from the pineclad slopes of the northern hemisphere.

Opposite: Trees in Australia florish in the harsh climatic conditions of the arid inland this gum rises against a backdrop of the Flinders Ranges.

Above: Trees sillouetted against the skyline on Tasmania's east coast.

Banksia

Boronia

Trigger flowers (Stylidium)

Guinea flower (Hibbertia)

trees, are generally found along the perimeter of the forest areas — like buffer zones between forests and the open grasslands. The type and extent of forests depends largely on rainfall — most are found where annual precipitation ranges between 1000 and 2500 millimetres per year.

Like the animals of this unusual country, much of the vegetation of Australia is unlike that of anywhere else. Indeed, the landing site of Captain Cook's *Endeavour* in 1770 was soon changed from "Stingray Harbour" to "Botany Bay" after a large number of plants were collected there by Joseph Banks, the naturalist of the expedition. Of some 500 species of eucalypts, only seven occur outside Australia — and most of those are in New Guinea. More than half the world's acacias are Australian wattles which differ markedly from the acacias of tropical America and Africa. There are about 12,000 flowering plants in Australia with the main families including Eucalyptus, Acacia, Banksia, Melaleuca and Casuarina.

Forests can be divided into three general categories — rainforests, wet open forests and dry open forests.

Rainforests are also known as closed forests because the top canopy blocks out 70 percent or more of sunlight to the ground. Most of the trees in rainforests are evergreens but sun-loving trees like eucalypts don't predominate. Many rainforests occupy only small areas so they often don't appear on large scale maps. There are rainforests thoughout eastern Australia from Cape York through to Tasmania as well as some at the top of Western Australia and the Northern Territory. They occur at any altitude between sea level and 1200 metres. Only those north of the Tropic of Capricorn are "tropical rainforests" — the rest on the mainland are "subtropical" or "warm temperate" rainforests. Tasmania is unique in having a large area of cool temperate rainforests. The top half of Cape York

Opposite: The waratah is the floral emblem of NSW and can be seen in flower near the coast at the start of summer.

Russell Falls in the Mount Field National Park, Tasmania descends 40 metres over three tiers through a dense rainforest.

Top: The Tasmanian Grey Kangaroo, unlike its mainland counterpart, is in danger of extinction — conservation measures have been taken to help their survival.

Middle: The Tiger cat or Spotted-tailed Quoll (Dasyurus maculatus) can be distinguished from other quolls by the spots on its tail. Weighing up to 7 kg, it is one of Australia's largest carnivorous marsupials. Logging and land clearance has greatly reduced its native habitat throughout eastern Australia — more could condemn it to extinction.

Opposite, top: Tanin and other organic materials give the water flowing off Crater Peak in the Cradle Mountain region of Tasmania the colour of a strong cup of tea.

Lichens, mosses and fungi are all common rainforest inhabitants: on trees (opposite, bottom) or rocks (above, left) in the Cradle Mountain-Lake St Clair National Park

Left: pattern in ferns, New England.

Above: The Tasmanian Devil (Sarcophilus harrisii) produces a growl and screech out of all proportion to its size. Primarily a carrion eater, since the apparent extinction of the Tasmanian Tiger (or Thylacine), it is the largest Australian carnivorous marsupial. A few hundred years ago, this terrier-sized creature lived on the Australian mainland, too, but seems to have been rendered extinct by the dingo which didn't make it to Tasmania. Despite its ferocious growl and appearance, the Tasmanian Devil relies more on bluff and bluster than physical attack. Another blow to its image as a fearless predator is its awkward wobbling gait.

Peninsula and around Darwin have monsoonal rainforests — the mainly deciduous trees shed their leaves at the start of the Dry so visitors travelling tracks which are only open during the dry season may not even realise that they are passing through rainforest.

Monsoonal rainforests are the exception — most rainforests always remain dense, dark and damp: a mass of buttressed trees such as figs with lianas or woody vines hanging from their branches. Ferns and orchids make the most of the large quantities of decaying matter and many types flourish: elkhorns, staghorns and maidenhair, climbing ferns and bird's-nest ferns mix with large rock liles and diminutive orchids. Rainforest trees include red cedar, coachwood, blackbean and rosewood with coniferous softwoods including bunya, kauri and hoop pines. Then there are the predators like the strangler figs which begin life as seedlings on branches then drop roots to the ground and slowly enmesh the host trees in a cage of roots, killing it. Often the original tree rots away, leaving the column of roots standing free with a hollow core.

In all ways this is a jungle where survival is all. Nowhere is that more clear than on the forest floor. The seedlings of rainforest trees have extraordinary capacity to endure without the sunlight they need to grow. When one of the giant canopy trees dies and falls, light streams in through the gap it leaves in the canopy and the seedlings battle to monopolise the light striking the floor of the forest. Eventually one assumes ascendancy and in its shade the others die.

There are about 600 species of mosses in Australia but only about 50 are unique to the country. They range from some so tiny that they can hardly be seen with the naked eye while the *Dawsonia superba* of the Australian rainforest can be 60 centimetres high. Mosses are fairly evenly divided between ground dwellers and those that grow on rocks or trees — the latter often draped from the branches. They need a wet, or at least damp, environment which is why they are found growing best on the shaded or southern side of trees in Australia (and the

Above: The Masked Owl (Tyto novaeholladiae).

Opposite, top: Horseshoe Falls Mt Field National Park, Tasmania

Opposite bottom: The rainforests surrounding the Cradle Mountain are wonderlands of rich vegetation and sparkling mountain streams.

Top: Knyvet Falls below Cradle Mountain Lodge.

Opposite: White-lipped tree frog (Litoria intrafrenata) found in North Quensland rainforests.

Top: Red eyed tree frogs (Litoria Chloris) embracing, Mary River.

Middle: Dainty Green tree frog (Litoria gracilenta), found along the Queensland/NSW coast.

Bottom: A Red eyed tree frog (Litoria Chloris) calling.

northern side in the northern hemisphere.)

The richest growths of fungi are in rainforest areas, too. Unlike other plants, fungi lack chlorophyll so they can't photosynthesise the sun's energy into food. Instead they have to take their food from other living or dead organisms. There are well over 100,000 types of fungi of which the best known (and most common of the large fungi) are mushrooms and toadstools but others can appear as gelatinous, leathery, spongy or wood-like in texture. Ghost fungus (*Pleurotus lampas*) found around the base of Australian trees or the delicate tropical *Hiatula wynniae* glow quite brightly in the dark. Some puffball fungi explode to spread their spores and it's been estimated that a single large puffball may contain seven thousand billion spores.

The characteristic Australian forest is the open or sclerophyll forest dominated by one or more types of eucalypts. "Sclerophyll" merely means that the tree has tough leaves which retain moisture well — a handy feature in areas of low or erratic rainfall. The canopy foliage obscures only 30 to 70 percent of the sun — considerably less than in rainforests. Wet sclerophyll forests are the most complex ones with the tallest trees — below the canopy (which often exceeds 30 metres in height) is a dense layer of lower trees and tall shrubs. The dominant eucalypt depends on location — in the southwest corner of WA it's often karri *(E. diversicolor)*, in Victoria or Tasmania it's mountain ash *(E. regnans)* and elsewhere on the east coast it may be Sydney blue gum *(E. saligna)*. The karri and mountain ash often predominate to the exclusion of other eucalypts whereas the others frequently occur surrounded by other types. Mountain ash 100 metres or more in height have been recorded placing them as the tallest trees in Australia and among the tallest in the world — the karri of Western Australia reach similar heights. These are the world's tallest hardwood trees.

Eucalypts are more commonly referred to as "gum trees" — a term used since soon after the arrival of the First Fleet. In a dispatch of May 15, 1788 Governor Phillip wrote "What seeds could be collected are sent to Sir Joseph Banks, as likewise the red gum taken from the large gum tree by tapping". The tannic, amber gum which led to the name is found in pockets within the timber and hardens on exposure to air. The name "eucalypt" comes from a Greek word meaning "covered" — referring to the cap which covers the flower until it is ready to bloom.

In locations where the rainfall is lower, dry sclerophyll forests may flourish. Again, there is often a high layer of eucalypts: typically red stringybark *(E. macroryhyncha)* in the east and jarrah *(E. marginata)* in the west. The lower layer is often Acacia and Casuarina in such forests. However, where the rainfall is less again, lower Acacia open forests may occur — with an underlayer of still shorter trees and shrubs and very little ground cover. Like eucalypts, Australian acacias are rarely referred to by their generic name — they are more commonly called "wattles". The word stems from early settlers' wattle-and-daub huts which used the wood of an unrelated (but similar looking) plant, Callicoma, in the frame work.

The history of forestry in Australia is a sorry one. In the main, the early settlers regarded the forests of Australia as an impediment to progress — to be removed by axe and fire as quickly as possible. Sawmillers were granted leases at fixed, nominal rates — some of these leases continued into the 1950's. However, as competition for the best timber areas increased, the government came to look on the forests as a source of revenue and only then gave a thought to the need to perpetuate this income. Minimum circumferences were declared but these were low enough not to interfere with loggers' selection and didn't effectively take into

Opposite, top: New England National Park, NSW.

Middle: The top canopy of the Washpool rainforest cuts out much of the light to the forest floor. When a tall tree falls, saplings and ground cover compete for the new patch of sunlight at groundlevel.

Flowers in the Blue Gum Forest, Grose Valley, NSW.

Top: Early morning, as the mist rises from the rainforest, is a magical time as the forest comes to life for the new day.

Opposite: Bearded dragon (Pogona barbatus) Eastern Australia.

Top: Hawkmoth just emerged from puppae, Sydney.
Left: Goanna (Varanus varius) in the Blue Gum Forest, NSW.
Right: A Short-beaked Echidna (Tachyglossus aculeatus) near Cradle Mountain, Tasmania.
Echidnas, with their pelt of fur and spines are found throughout Australia. They are also known
as Spiny Anteaters — they eat ants by sticking their saliva coated tongues down ant nests then
mashing the takings between horny pads in their mouths.

deciduous beech (Nothofagus gunnii), Tas

Pigface (Carpobrotus), WA

Diplarrena, Cradle Mountain, Tas
Tea tree, New England, NSW

Tea tree (Leptospermum), NSW
Native milkwort (Comesperma), NSW

Lichen, cool temperate rainforest, Tas

Carnivorous sundews (Drosera)

Gristle fern (Gleichenia), NSW
Rice flower (Pimelea), New England

Exposed roots, Cradle Mountain, Tas
pattern in fallen gum leaves

account the variable growth rate of the same species under different conditions.

Authorities exhibited a lack of ability to come to terms with the Australian environment, importing and planting species which shouldn't have been introduced while other species were planted in the wrong places. In an effort to emulate the orderly forests of Europe, local forests were cleared of undergrowth leading to erosion and, by encouraging grass to grow, increasing the chance of forest fires. Under a program of "assisted regeneration" many trees not commercially exploited at the time were ringbarked — a wanton waste of diminishing natural resources.

Today there is continuing conflict between the economic necessities of providing timber and the more far-reaching need to ensure the continued survival of the Australian bush. It is an issue wherever there are forests left in Australia. Already many species have been cut to near extinction. Less than half the rainforests in NSW have survived the last 200 years — those that have are either part of National Parks or under threat of logging or being cleared for pastoral expansion. When the first European settlers arrived less than one percent of Australia was rainforest — only a quarter of that one percent still remains. In NSW, Victoria and Tasmania, large swaths of forests have been clear-felled to be sold overseas as wood chips. Australian Newsprint Mills at Boyer on the Derwent River, Tasmania supplies about 40% of Australia's newsprint requirements — largely from the huge mountain ash growing on its 160,000 hectare forest concession. The mill came into operation in 1940.

Australia's climate and vegetation were not always as they are today.

Pines and the other conifers became established on all continents because when they came into existence the continents were joined together. By the time of the flowering plants around 90 million years ago, continental separation was largely completed so species were much more localised. Australia started to split with Antarctica some 55 million years ago and began its drift northwards towards its current position.

At this time, Australia's inland regions were becoming drier so trees were forced to adapt or die. By 30 million years ago, both wattles and eucalypts were recognisable groups. Unlike overseas acacias, Australian wattles have leaves reduced to flattened and enlarged leaf stalks which functioned like leaves but were better suited to arid conditions. Eucalypts came from myrtles but while the modern myrtle of the tropical Americas has a soft fruit, eucalypts have hard gumnuts. Over the years, Australian vegetation (now isolated from other continents) continued to evolve into the many unique plants we have today. One of the surprising adaptations was the tolerance many Australian trees developed to fires — indeed many depend upon fires to trigger the new generations.

Although Torres Strait is a clear dividing line between the plants of Australia and those of South East Asia, it is clear that there has been some crossover during the past 10 million years or so. Most likely, seeds have been carried on ocean currents or by migratory birds. Of course, the most effective transfer has been in places where climates and conditions are similar. Many rainforest plants of the Indo-Malayan region are now well established in the northern rainforests of Australia — just as there are eucalypts in New Guinea.

About 10 million years ago, Australian beech forests largely lost out to eucalypts. Woodlands and grasslands first appeared then expanded rapidly about three million years ago — in the mountains above the tree-line and in arid areas where even hardy eucalypts and wattles couldn't flourish. As conditions became more arid about two million years ago, rainforests shrank too — into ever smaller regions along the east coast.

Forests are remarkably complex structures. Although an apparent random collection of individual vegetation and fauna, in many ways a forest forms a single entity.

Opposite: The face of an Emperor Gum Moth (male) just emerged from cocoon seen below it.

Top: The Koala (Phascolarctos cinereus) takes all the moisture it needs from the leaves it eats. Its name is Aboriginal and translates as "no drinking".

Bottom: Goannas are accomplished climbers and often take to the trees to avoid pursuit. The pattern on their skin can make them very difficult to spot against the bark of some trees.

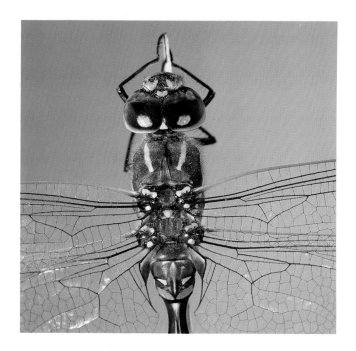

Opposite: Unlike the surrounding countryside of inland southern Queensland, Carnarvon Gorge contains a permanent water supply.

Top, left: A Dragonfly.
Top, right: an Emeror Gum Moth (Antheraea eucalypti).
Left: A young tree fern shoot uncoiling, Border Ranges Park, Northern NSW.

Overleaf:
page 82: Purling Brook Falls, Lamington National Park, Queensland.

Page 83

Top: A Golden tail gecko (Diplodactus taenicauda) in a cypress forest, South West Queensland.
Middle, left: A Gum-leaf moth of South East Queensland.
Middle, right: A Hooded scaly-foot lizard (pygopus migriceps) in a defensive pose, near Roma, southern Queensland.
Bottom, left: A Tree cricket (chlorobalius leucoviridis) in native cypress forests, Queensland.
Bottom, right: A leaf tail gecko (phyllurus cornutus) threatening, Mount Tambourine, Queensland.

It is impossible to forecast the ultimate result of changing or removing a single element of the forest. We have come a long way since it seemed reasonable to clear the scrub from Australian native forests so they would more closely resemble the plantations of Europe but complete understanding is not yet in sight. In the interim, we seem prepared to risk the long term future of many forests for a quick profit.

The isolation in which Australian forests developed has been shattered by European settlement of the country. Burning and clearing have been only the two most obvious ways we have destroyed Australian forests — and, through the resulting erosion, the usefulness of the land. Introducing exotic plants and bringing in non-native animals may have effects equally far reaching. The widespread use of fertilisers has also played a part. It has been observed in National Parks near or within cities that the nitrogen balance has been dramatically altered by water run-off laden with garden fertiliser.

Over the past 200 years Australia has altered more than it has in the past 10 million years. One effect of an increasingly high technology, urbanised society is that we are coming to appreciate our natural environment more and more. One can only hope that by the time we realise forests are necessities not luxuries there will still be some native forests left in Australia.

Above: detail in a tree trunk, Myall Lakes, NSW.

Top: A Mainland Tigersnake (Notechis scutatus) — found in Victoria, NSW, South Australia and South Queensland.

Above: A Bird spider from Atherton Tablelands.

Left: Wombats (Vombatus ursinus) are more closely related to Koalas than any other marsupial. Usually only one baby is born.

Previous page: Hairpin banksia (Banksia spinulosa).
Opposite: Grass Tree (Xanthorrhoea australis).

Above: Baeckea ramosissima
Left: Mountain Grevillea (Grevillea alpina).

Above: Katherine Gorge, Northern Territory at sunset.
Opposite, top: Tunnel Creek in the Kimberleys of Western Australia, lies on the same fossilised reef as Geikie Gorge. The creek originally flowed along the surface but wore away a joint fracture in the limestone to form a tunnel over half a kilometre long. Light streams into the tunnel from where the roof collapsed near the centre of the tunnel.

Bottom, left: All the eucalypts found in Western Australia are found nowhere else. The tallest is the karri (Eucalyptus diversicolor) of southwest Western Australia — one of the greatest hardwoods and in the running for the world's tallest tree. In 1901, a karri was cut down which measured 104 metres. The Guiness Book of Records states that the tallest tree in the world is a Californian coastal redwood at 111.6 metres in 1970.

Bottom, right: The series of 13 gorges which together make up Katherine Gorge rise up to 100 metres above the river — and extend for 12 kilometres like beads along a necklace.

Above: Kanangra Walls, Blue Mountains, NSW. Opposite: Stirling Ranges, Southern WA.

Mountains

Opposite: The MacDonnell Ranges in The Centre are very often described as "ancient" because their weatherworn folds look tired and the rounded slopes give an impression of immense age. In fact, ranges such as the Hamersleys in the north are much older. The MacDonnell Ranges were pushed up about 300 million years ago.

Above: With a maximum height of 500 metres, it isn't altitude which makes the MacDonnell Ranges of the Northern Territory, special — although they still provide great relief against the flatness of the surrounding plains. Rather, it is the gorges carved over millions of years by the rivers flowing through them in ages past: no stream has been perennial over the past 20,000 years. The cross-sections of rock revealed in the gorges provides an insight into the formation of the continent. In the 1870's, it became important to find a pass through the MacDonnell Ranges to put the overland telegraph line through and set up a telegraph station. Heavitree Gap was discovered in 1871 and the dry riverbed was named after the Postmaster-General, Todd and the spring within was named after his wife, Alice. Within years, many of the nearby canyons were home to herds of sheep and cattle as settlers followed the explorers.

Below: Hibiscus in the MacDonnell Ranges.

It was fortunate that the weather was cool in May. Indeed the air was cooler as the walkers climbed higher into the mountains. But that was more than offset by the hard work required to get there — no trails and dense bush is a hard combination at any time but cliff faces and no maps made this journey exceptionally difficult. There were seven in the party and it had been a week since they left the last point of civilisation.

At first it had been easy — a stroll through forest but across level ground. But after the river, the only way to go had been up. They were still climbing a week later. And now it looked like the end of the road. All the days of scrub bashing and apparent progress had brought then to this point — the end of an escarpment. Unless they could scramble down from here to continue westwards they would have to retreat and admit defeat. Without the horses the scramble would have posed few problems but, without the horses, they would never have reached this far. Even trying to take the horses down this slope with its loose scree and leg-snapping boulders was a calculated risk — they could ill-afford to lose one.

Several hours later, they were all standing at the base of the cliff. It had been a difficult descent but standing in this fertile valley with the way clear in front, the effort definitely seemed worthwhile. If immortality had been their goal — rather than finding new grazing land — this week's work put them among a select few whose names stand out in history. A century and more later, one of the few clear memories many Australian school children would retain from the classroom was that, in 1813, Blaxland, Lawson and Wentworth crossed the Blue Mountains. The four convicts with them never made it as far as the school history texts.

These days, the Blue Mountains is an easy day's excursion from Sydney.

Top: The Stirling Ranges are the only places in WA which ever experience snow.

Above: The Wedge-tailed Eagle (Aquila audax), the fourth largest in the world.

Drive up to Katoomba for lunch, walk for a few hours in the afternoon so one feels justified in having scones, jam and cream for afternoon tea then drive home in time for the Sunday night movie on television. More energetic visitors see the mountains on walking holidays, camping overnight and perhaps even crossing the route of those first three pathfinders. However, when Blaxland, Lawson and Wentworth found a way through this Great Dividing Range, they had carved a path deep into terra incognita — it had indeed been unknown territory until they showed it could be opened up.

Others had tried before. The first party set out in 1789, less than two years after the First Fleet had arrived in Botany Bay. They travelled about 22 kilometres into the hinterland beyond the Nepean River before turning back. Over the following years, numerous others tried and failed. They all returned to report that the same rough mountain terrain stretched far to the north and south and created "an impassable barrier" to the west. After George Caley's unsuccessful expedition of 1804, Governor King wrote: "As far as respects the extension of agriculture beyond the first range of mountains, that is an idea that must be given up, as the rocks to the west of that range wear the most barren and forbidding aspect, which men, animals, birds and vegetation have ever been strangers to, a better proof of which may not be adduced than the remark of one of Caley's party in returning who exclaimed, on seeing two solitary crows, that 'they had lost their way'".

The real achievement of the 1813 expedition was not crossing the main range — they only reached the Cox River and it was up to George Evans to completely cross the Great Dividing Range later that year when he extended their route past the site of what is now Bathurst. No, their place in history is deserved for finding a

way through the most difficult section — the rugged, deeply cut Blue Mountains which had foiled the best efforts for 25 years. Blaxland, the leader of the expedition, achieved this by continually following the ridge tops rather than being diverted down into the valleys below.

Mountains are the most predominant landforms in nature's whole wonderful array of features. No matter the beauty of the foreground, one's eyes are always drawn towards the peaks, however distant. In this regard, Australia appears to miss out as it has a singular lack of high peaks. The highest point on the continent, Mt Kosciusko at 2225 metres is a mere molehill in comparison with Asia's Mt Everest which rises to 8848 metres. Every other continent (including Antarctica) has at least one peak over 5000 metres high.

Australia is remarkably flat, too. There is not just an absence of peaks but the overall terrain is largely smooth. That doesn't mean that it is all lowlands — Australia's mean altitude of 330 metres is more than that of Europe alone (290 metres) but less than the other continents: South America (650 metres), Africa (660 metres), North America (780 metres), Asia/Europe combined (860 metres) and Antarctica (2,200 metres). Australia has less plateau area above 1,000 metres than any other continent and only South America has a lower proportion of coastal plains — our plains consist of low to medium altitude plateaux.

However, Australia's mountains, while few and low, have a surprisingly rugged grandeur. This is the result of deep valleys and gorges being carved in them over the ages. The low profile of the Blue Mountains as seen from the Sydney basin suggests relatively gentle hills — an appearance belied by the experience of the early explorers. Standing at Echo Point, Katoomba the view down into the Jamison Valley far below is very impressive — exceptionally so in

Top: Simpsons Gap National Park is only eight kilometres west of Alice Springs, NT.

Above: The Flinders Ranges, SA were formed about 500 million years ago when the rock layers, originally laid down under the sea, were thrust up in a violent earth movement.

Above: Wilpena Pound, the result of folding of the earth's strata, has the highest point in the Flinders Ranges SA — St Mary Peak, 1165 metres.

late afternoon or dawn. The deepest valley in Australia is Geehi: the river flows 1700 metres below the high peaks of the main Snowy Mountains range — Mt Kosciusko and Mt Townsend (2210 metres) which are only a few kilometres away.

So it is that the flattest, driest continent has some of the highest waterfalls in the world. Wollombombi Falls in the New England Ranges of NSW has a drop of 472 metres making it the fifth highest in the world. The name of the falls is a corruption of the local Aboriginal name "Wallamumbi" meaning "great falls". Wallaman Falls on Stony Creek, a tributary of the Herbert River near Ingham, Queensland are the second highest at 350 metres. Of course the water flow over these falls is insignificant by comparison with the mind-numbing force of the Victoria Falls of Africa and Niagara in North America but the depth of the chasms into which they fall is inspiring. Still, in the wet season, the daily flow of Barron Falls in the Atherton Tablelands used to be 2 366 million litres a day — a total annual flow enough to twice fill Sydney Harbour. However, since the construction of Tinaroo Dam, the falls are now only an overflow spillway which flow only during the wet season.

It is sometimes difficult to grasp how unusual Australia really is and how the creation of the landscape we see today is at such great variance from elsewhere in the world. To a great extent, glaciers are the chalk and erasers which shape and re-shape the blank slate of continents into landforms. The last great ice age which modelled much of Europe and North America only 25,000 years ago didn't change the face of Australia. Rather, Australia as we see it today has come about over 250 million years — since the Permian ice sheets which covered a large part of Australia. It is truly an ancient continent.

Because of the time scale difference, factors which went into the shaping of

Top: Layers of mountains and mist, Southwest coast of Tasmania.

Above: Lake Pedder as it now appears is the result of a conservation battle lost. The Gordon River Dam was built by the Tasmanian Government despite strong protests that a beautiful and unusual white quartzite sand beach would be drowned.

Cradle Mountain-Lake St Clair National Park is the best known of Tasmania's wilderness areas and the one which provides the easiest access to the rugged mountain splendour of the island State. It is an area of towering dolerite peaks (including the highest in Tasmania — Mt Ossa, 1617 metres), alpine grasses and moorlands, beech forests and snow gums. The region is populated by Tasmanian devils, wombats, echidnas, marsupial "cats" and platypuses. Although Mt Kosciusko and the Snowy Mountains are higher, the more southern Tasmanian central alps encapsulate Australia's mountain scenery at its most stark. The 85 kilometre walking track from the shores of Lake Dove under the peak of Cradle Mountain to Lake St Clair attracts hikers from all over the world. Even in the middle of summer, the weather can shift without warning from warm sunny skies to mist and snow (opposite). The vegetation along the way ranges from flower covered bushes and trees (top left) to water-sodden mosses (top right). The northern end of the park — around Cradle Valley and Crater Peak (top middle) — is the more rugged, tapering down somewhat towards Lake St Clair. The Park was included on the World Heritage List in 1982.

Right: Staghorn fern
(Platycerium grande).
Top: The top of Bald Rock, an
immense granite dome outside
Tenterfield, northern NSW, is
1341 metres above sea level and
stands 200 metres above the
surrounding gum forests.
At 750 metres long and
500 metres wide, Bald Rock is
the second largest monolith on
earth. Unlike Ayers Rock, from
the top climbers have views over
the New England highlands to
the coast.
Above: Like a Henry Moore
figure, this weatherworn dead
tree in the Cradle Valley
continues to reach a branch
towards the sky.

Above: Bogong National Park contains 11 of Victoria's 12 highest peaks with the tallest, Mt Bogong (1986 metres) standing in solitary splendour in the northern corner. The whole of the Bogong high plains lies above the winter snowline

Opposite, top: cloud in Kanangra Valley, NSW. Opposite, bottom: Snowgums, Bogong National Park.

Australia have long since been erased in other places of the world. It is hard to imagine how different things have been at the various stages of Australia's development. Landforms we see today were being started when most of the world's land masses were clustered together in a single lump called Pangaea. The northern coast of WA has been coastal for 600 million years but the Perth Basin was part of the interior of the supercontinent of Gondwanaland until about 100 million years ago when Africa and India split from Australia/Antarctica and each other. Tasmania was close to the South Pole until about 65 million years ago — anyone caught in a summer snowstorm on the Cradle Mountain — Lake St Clair trail may argue that it's still too close.

The Permian ice sheets erased whatever landforms previously existed. They swept from the south depositing glacial detritus as far north as northern Queensland. What is now the east coast was a series of marine basins and volcanic islands — the marine basins are now important sources of coal. By about 225 million years ago, Australia was nearly all land. Around 150 million years ago thousands of cubic kilometres of dolerite spurted through the sediment layers of Tasmania — perhaps a precursor of the forthcoming rupture between Antarctica and Australia. The mountains of Tasmania still feature large dolerite sections.

In the Cretaceous period (136 million to 65 million years ago) there was worldwide flooding as ocean levels rose. The rising waters divided Australia into three landmasses (southwest, northwest/central and eastern seaboard) — about

one third of Australia has a layer of Cretaceous rocks although in many places they are covered by later deposits. As the sea withdrew, many of the river systems of today were established.

Australia consists of three major structures: the Western Shield (or Great Western Plateau) which covers most of Western Australia and the Northern Territory and a large part of South Australia; the Central Basin (or Interior Lowlands) running north-south from the Gulf to the south-east coast of South Australia; and the Eastern Uplands which runs along the east coast taking in Tasmania and much of Victoria.

The Western Shield is a plateau which is, on average about 400 metres high and covers two thirds of Australia. It is made up of very ancient rocks (and ore deposits) — zircons found in Western Australia date back to just over four billion years ago when the earth was first being formed. Although largely flat the Shield does have some highlands: the Stirling, Hamersley, Kimberley and King Leopold ranges of WA, Arnhem Escarpment, MacDonnell and Murchison ranges of the NT, Barkly Tablelands of Queensland, the Flinders Ranges of SA and the Barrier Range of western NSW are all part of it.

The Central Basin is three great basins separated by low ranges. There are no mountains of note in this region unlike the Eastern Uplands which has most of Australia's mountains. The upland is a plateau of varying height from less than 300 metres to the highlands of the Snowy Mountains, Victorian Alps, New England Tablelands and the mountains of Tasmania. The highlands generally

slope steeply to the east coast while the western slopes are much gentler.

The Eastern Uplands are the result of both volcanic and tectonic activity so their structure is very complex. Australia has no active volcanoes and is earthquake-free in comparison with much of the world — particularly its near Pacific neighbours. That's because Australia is located towards the centre of its "plate" which extends to cover India and New Zealand, too. This is a much more stable place to be than on the edge of a plate (as New Zealand is) or poised over the junction of two plates like San Francisco. However, the position didn't keep Australia immune from subterranean activity: Mt Gambier in SA erupted only 1400 years ago.

Over the millenia, Australia's volcanic activity extended throughout the whole of the Eastern Uplands but it was indicative of the geological forces which gave rise to the Uplands rather than the main formative elements. Volcanoes are clear signs that the fabric of the earth is under   stress — these forces may be vented either by volcanic eruption or tectonic uplifting or folding. This shaping of the continent took place throughout its development: uplifting some 350 million years ago raised the mountains of Tasmania and, later, the MacDonnell Ranges of Central Australia; the mountains from central Queensland down to New England, NSW were thrown up about 310 million years ago and substantially added to 225 million years ago. In the Oligocene epoch from 37 million to 22 million years ago, the Himalayas, European Alps and Rocky Mountains/Andes ranges were formed. Australia experienced substantial volcanic activity too. The volcanic plugs of the Warrumbungles and Mt Warning in northern NSW and the Glasshouse

Above:From the air, the Snowy Mountains main range can be seen as a solid, smooth wall. Winter winds hit this wall and are thrown high over it. This photograph was taken by Richard Bassett from a tiny single-seater fibreglass glider at an altitude of 25,000 feet, soaring the mountain wave.

Top: Ruined Castle is an outcrop of basaltic vertical columns in Bogong National Park frequently covered by snow. Opposite: Richea pandaniflora is a giant heath which grows up to 10 metres in height and looks more suited to a tropical rainforest than Bogong snow country.

Above: The Grampians National Park is Victoria's biggest and, established in 1984, one of the most recently declared. The Grand Canyon (pictured) is formed by the etching of rain and chemical action against the ridges of the Serra Range.

Opposite, top: The rainbow effect created by sunlight being broken down into the spectrum is caused by ice crystals in clouds. This cloud was above Jindabyne in winter.

Opposite, left: Even weeds in an alpine field take on an appealing air when dusted by frost, Jindabyne, NSW.

Opposite, right: An undercut ledge provides a spectacular view of the Grampians, Victoria.

Mountains of southern Queensland are reminders of this volcanic age. However, it was the last major uplift less than two million years ago that formed the east coast mountains we see today. This was the Kosciusko Uplift which created the Great Dividing Range. A later Ice Age carved the glaciated peaks and cirques around Mt Kosciusko and the mountains of Tasmania. Lake St Clair in Tasmania, a lake 172 metres deep, is the result of glacial gouging but the relatively small glaciers of Tasmania were not sufficient to reach the sea with the power to form fiords.

The incredible duration over which the mountains of Australia were formed gives the continent a variety in its mountain scenery which is unique. Sharp dolerite and quartzite peaks of western Tasmania and the rounded slopes of the MacDonnell Ranges in Central Australia are as unlike as mountains can be. The Stirling Ranges rise tier on tier from the southern plains of Western Australia whereas the Arnhem Escarpment is a single step from the floodplains below. Climate, too — both directly and through its effect on vegetation — has a marked effect on the mood generated by each mountain range. The lush rainforests of the Atherton Tablelands are at similar latitude to the bush of Kakadu but the sunlit palms and ferns of the latter are at variance to sombre trails under the dense rainforest canopy past giant figs and vaguely threatening loops of strangler vine. Watching a grey kangaroo emerge from the heavy mists of the dense New England forests is unlike watching the sun burn the mist off buttongrass plains high above the treeline of Cradle Mountain or Kosciusko.

Some of the most spectacular mountain scenes take place high above the peaks of Kosciusko and the Main Range. Many visitors to the area fail to notice the special cloud displays created over the ranges by the winter winds. Over the past few years, the Alpine Soaring Centre in Jindabyne, run by gliding instructor Barry Wrenford, has explored the winds over the mountains in sleek fibreglass gliders.

for their bizarre shapes, the Bungles would be worth visiting. However, the original sandstone was laid down in vertical bands. As water has seeped into it and out again, it has deposited a hard skin on the outside of the fragile sandstone. From some layers, the coating is orange from silica in the rock while the outside of others is black from an organic growth. The overall effect is of hundreds of rock cones in contrasting black and orange tiger stripes. In the area around the towers and the deep gorges cut through the massif itself there are palm-shaded waterholes, caves as large as cathedrals, rocky creek beds and picturesque sandy beaches glowing red from the sunlight off the cliff walls.

The whole spectacular formation covers several hundred square kilometres and, as yet, there have been few visitors. It is one of the most unusual natural attractions in the world and it says a lot about the vastness of Australia that it was only this decade that more than a handful of people heard about it. Every year the number of visitors to the area is many times that of the previous year. The West Australia government is acting to protect Bungle Bungle within a National Park to be run in conjunction with the traditional owners.

Bungle Bungle has the potential to draw as many — or more — visitors than Ayers Rock but the rock crust which makes it special is wafer-thin. Each footstep does irreparable damage and leaves the towers open to extensive erosion in the monsoonal deluges of the wet season. It would be very easy to love the Bungles to death but they are too special to fall back into obscurity again — even for their own protection. Administering the Bungle Bungle National Park will reveal how far we have come towards learning to protect the treasures of the Australian wilderness.

Opposite: The Bungle Bungle massif in an isolated region of the far north of WA is one of the most astounding areas in Australia, a continent of superlative landforms.

Top, left: Anthills can closely resemble neighbouring Bungle Bungle towers.

Top, right: the bull's eye pattern at the top of a Bungle Bungle tower clearly shows the horizontal black (algal) and orange (silica) banding on the surface of the sandstone. Loose rocks on the top of the towers have been released from the conglomerate by weathering.

Above: In this harsh environment, survival is all. This prickly nightshade even has thorns on the petals of its flowers!

Opposite: Piccaninny Gorge, Bungle Bungle.

Cork tree.

This deep hole in the sandstone of Bungle Bungle is the result of water action on the fragile sandstone of the massif.

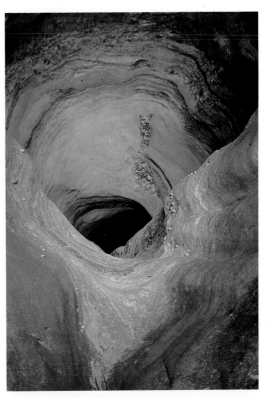

Bottom, left: Wherever there is a regular water supply in Bungle Bungle, there is vegetation.

Bottom, right: Nature mimics nature: this antnest has perfectly reproduced the form of the baobab tree found in the area.

Above: Sandstorm over Lake Eyre, SA.

Deserts

Above: The sandstorm seen overleaf approaches, Lake Eyre, SA.

Opposite, top: Dust storms are a major form of erosion in desert areas.

Opposite, middle: Wolf Creek meteorite crater, the second largest in the world, is only one of several in Australia but the desert climate has preserved it exceptionally well.

Opposite, bottom: Once Lake Mungo in the far west of NSW had a much wetter, more hospitable history than it does now and supported a great variety of wildlife. The earliest inhabitants of Australia lived here, too: evidence of human habitation dates back almost 40,000 years — one of the very earliest in the world. Mungo National Park is a World Heritage area — these eroded sands may hold many secrets from the beginnings of mankind.

Opposite: Fluffy, individual cumulus clouds are clear indicators of strong thermal activity as the sun-heated earth heats the air above it which in turn forms clouds when it rises high enough to cool and condense. In the desert, where there are no landforms to interfer, the wind often arranges the thermals into "streets" running in the same direction as the wind

Right: Drying mud on the floor of a river bed forms interesting geometric patterns but may also signal doom to the creatures depending on it for survival.

It had been less than a day since we left the small South Australian settlement of Arkaroola. Within the folds of the Flinders Ranges, dawn light revealed stunted trees, thorny grass and dried creek beds between rocky, rounded hills. The sun was now setting on that same day but there was not a tree or hill to provide a lengthening shadow. Instead, we had an uninterrupted view of a straight horizon in all directions. Until about midday, our journey had been accompanied by the tail end of the ranges but they were finally reduced to a series of hillocks which proved unequal to the vastness of the desert and these, too faded away to nothing.

Out here, it was hard not to feel overwhelmed by the immensity of the sky above and the apparent lack of progress over a barren plain. However, a lump appeared against the sky to the north and soon resolved into a windmill with a homestead nearby. We stopped to ponder how anyone could eke a living out of the desolate land in which we stood. The last sign of human habitation had been more than 50 kilometres before and since then we had seen no sign of a living thing except the handiwork of those who put in the ribbon of road we were following. No cattle or other stock, none of the kangaroos and emus one finds along the fringes of the desert, not even a skink or lizard scurrying to the side of the track at our passing. "Maybe it's a pet rock farm" Trevor surmised. We turned in at the gate.

The station owner came out to greet us. Leaning over the fence between the green homestead yard and the dusty, pebbly desert he mentioned that we were only the last of several visitors to call in that day. That everyone stopped wasn't surprising — we were entering the desolation of The Centre where travellers are expected to report their presence at every house so they can be located if a vehicle breaks down leaving them stranded. However, the number of callers was unusual — if there were many vehicles (and several in a single day constitutes a veritable traffic jam) the process of "logging in" becomes superfluous. I asked if he considered it essential for us to call at the next homestead, interrupting proceedings there, too. The owner looked at the featureless landscape stretching to infinity, grinned and stated "What next homestead? After you leave here, mate, you're out of the suburbs".

That conversation took place several years ago on an early excursion I made travelling the Strezlecki track by motorcycle. Since then, there have been many trips into the heart of Australia from various points along the coast. From the

vantage point of urban Australia huddled along the fringes of the continent, the desert is merely the hazy and unknown centre which, in ages past, would have been dismissed with a map notation of "terra incognita" or perhaps "here be tygers".

Those who take the time to explore the many different deserts within Australia find a wealth of wilderness which is rapidly becoming a focal point to our burgeoning tourist industry. True, many parts are crossed by tracks of seismic vehicles but these are only minor sullies though, when encountered, they detract greatly from the feeling that you are the first to venture far enough the reach this place. In fact, the deserts are the buffers which ensure Australia will never be covered by cities and factories, or manicured fields and gardens, as so many other countries are. The harsh land under a merciless sun has been tamed enough to allow occasional forays into its depths but it resists most attempts of permanent habitation. Indeed, travellers beneath the cobalt blue sky often pass deserted homesteads and out-stations, crumbling like the dreams they were made from.

The deserts of Australia extend over five million square kilometres — about one third of the continent. They are next in size only to the Sahara which covers a massive 6.7 million square kilometres. By comparison, the deserts of Arabia are

less than half the size of those in Australia and the Kalahari, Gobi, Colorado and Thar desert are tiny. Of course, scientists have long argued over what is a desert: should it be determined on the rainfall, what can be grown there and whether people can profitably live there? One of the most influential of early Australian geographers, Griffith Taylor writing in 1940, split "Empty Australia" into "Sparselands" and "Deserts", the division being basically those areas where people survive off the land and the areas where this is highly unlikely. In support, he quotes Gregory (1909) who defines a desert as "a country with such an arid climate and such scanty water supply that agriculture is impractical and occupation is found possible only for a sparse population of pastoralists". That's the most practical definition of a desert — if it's too dry to graze, it's desert. However, many areas which could be settled remain wilderness and even in regions where animals do graze, there are pockets of wilderness because people and their herds have yet to change it. And there are several areas of desert which must be preserved as wilderness for the natural features or outstanding natural beauty — deserts are far from being uniform nothingness.

Some of the world's deserts are the results of rainshadows. Tibet is a clear example — the clouds sweeping in from India strike the high Himalayas and dump their moisture in Nepal, leaving Tibet parched and dusty less than one

Left: The Simpson desert which extends into Queensland, NT and SA, covers an area twice the size of Tasmania. The predominant landforms are sand ridges, 30 metres high, about 500 metres apart and stretching for up to 300 kilometres north and south.

Previous pages: page 128-29 The Olgas, NT.

Page 130-31 The Devils Marbles, NT.

Opposite: Weano Gorge, Hamersley Range, WA.

Right: Sturt's desert pea (Clianthus formosus), the floral emblem of South Australia, is named after Charles Sturt (1795-1869), the explorer who did much to open up the centre of the continent.

hundred kilometres away. However, the deserts of Australia are, like the Sahara, the product of the Trade Winds and the dry weather patterns formed over inland Australia. Although from the air, there is an occasional impression of treelined streams, approached from the ground these can be seen to be hardy trees growing along dry waterbeds awaiting rare cloudbursts and sustaining themselves meanwhile by dropping roots down to sub-artesian streams.

About 70 percent of Australia is arid — the whole continent has less rainfall than any other while its rate of evaporation is among the highest in the world. The end result is that Australia has only a third the water runoff of Africa and less than 20 percent the rate of any other continent. This has given rise to an unusual drainage system—many rivers flow not to the coast but into a series of inland lakes from where the water evaporates.

The largest lake of inland Australia is Lake Eyre in South Australia. When it is full, it covers 15 000 square kilometres — receiving the drainage of an area of about one and a quarter million square kilometres. However, it is rarely filled — normally it is an expanse of saline mud capped with a thick salt crust. The rivers which flow into it rise in regions with low and intermittent rainfall and flow through areas which are even drier. The main streams feeding it are Eyre Creek, the Diamantina and Cooper Creek — all flow down very shallow gradients so that they form an intricate pattern of side branch streams which reform in the few sections where they flow through low valleys. These wide alluvial plains are the Channel Country. On the occasions when Lake Eyre is filled, the greatest depth is about four metres — it takes about four years for the water to evaporate away. At its lowest point, Lake Eyre is 12 metres below sea level. It was discovered by E. J. Eyre in 1840 who also had Eyre Peninsula named after him by South Australia's Governor Gawler.

Besides Lake Eyre, there are numerous other salt lakes in Central Australia — Lakes Gregory, Frome and Blanche are all fed by various impermanent tributaries. The Todd which rises in the MacDonnell Ranges and passes through

Opposite: The gibbers of Sturts Stony Desert, South Australia, shine like polished copper under a cloudless sky. Although the sight of this detritus (left behind from ancient uplands) stretching from one horizon to the other is initially fascinating, it provides an uncomfortable path for anyone attempting to cross it. As every traveller unfortunate enough to make camp here has found, the ground defeats any tent peg and the layers of rock can't be cleared or smoothed to make a halfway comfortable bed.

Above: The Dingo (Canis familiaris dingo) is one of an equitorial group of primitive dogs introduced into Australia by Aborigines sometime in the past few thousand years. Although rabbits and kangaroos from the bulk of its diet, the dingo's marauding against sheep gave rise to the world's longest fence: the "dingo fence" which runs through South Australia and into Queensland. It's held that the dingo was responsible for the decline of the Thylacine on the Australian mainland.

Opposite: Ayers Rock, the world's largest monolith, is close behind the Great Barrier Reef as the natural feature most visitors to Australia want to see. The immense walls of The Rock, rising sheer from the desert plains remain as inspiring today as they were when William Gosse described it in his 1873 diary as "certainly the most wonderful natural feature I have ever seen".

Top, left: The Thorny Devil (Molock horridus) of arid Australia.

Top, right: The remarkably monochromatic Desert banded snake (Simoseleps bertholdi).

Above: The smooth white trunk of a Ghost gum (Eucalyptus papuana) against the Devils Marbles, NT.

Alice Springs continues onto oblivion among the sand ridges of the Simpson Desert.

If there is a river which embodies the spirit of Central Australia, it is the Cooper Creek. Banjo Paterson used it in *Clancy of the Overflow* as the representation of everything missing from city life:

> *"In my wild erratic fancy visions come to me of Clancy*
> *Gone a-droving 'down the Cooper' where the western drovers go;*
> *As the stock are slowly stringing, Clancy rides behind them singing,*
> *For the drover's life has pleasures that the townsfolk never know.*
> *And the bush has friends to meet him, and their kindly voices greet him.*
> *In the murmur of the breezes and the river on its bars,*
> *And he sees the vision splendid of the sunlit plain extended,*
> *And at night the wondrous glory of the everlasting stars."*

Cooper Creek is formed by the conjunction of the Barcoo River and Thomson River of the Channel Country. A much repeated joke of the region is that it takes two rivers to form Cooper Creek. It says much about the convoluted channel patterns and the absence of permanent waterways that it took almost a century to sort out the naming of this creek. Charles Sturt discovered it in August, 1845 and named it Cooper's Creek after Charles (later Sir Charles) Cooper, the first Chief Justice of South Australia. The 1958 edition of the *Australian Encyclopaedia* picks up the story from there:

The red earth and tussocks of the Pilbara, WA.

"Subsequently there was much controversy about the naming of the creek..(it)..followed A. C. Gregory's revelation (in 1858) that the stream which Sir Thomas Mitchell had named the Victoria, and which E. B. Kennedy had declared was called Barcoo by the aborigines, was in fact the upper course of the Cooper. Even so, there would have been no need to question the adaptation of Sturt's name for the creek, had it not been erroneously assumed that Mitchell's discovery was made in September 1845 instead of 1846 and that 'Victoria' therefore had priority. Finally, in 1860, the Secretary of State for the Colonies authorized the use of the name Barcoo for the entire course. Thereafter the stream was shown on maps with Barcoo River and Cooper's Creek as alternative names, and it was only about 80 years before the use of Barcoo only for that part which lies above the junction with the Thompson was generally adopted. It is now also the usual practice to omit the possessive 's' from the name Cooper's Creek."

In times of flood, the Cooper can be more than 80 kilometres wide as it flows towards Lake Eyre. However, such times are rare. More frequently, Cooper Creek dissipates into a series of shallow channels which fail to reach the Lake.

Near Cooper Creek is the famous "dig" tree of the ill-fated Burke and Wills overland expedition to cross the continent from south to north via the Darling River and Cooper Creek. The expedition left Melbourne in August 1860 and Cooper Creek in December of the same year. In April 1861, three of the expedition staggered back into Cooper Creek only seven hours after the relief

party (which had waited for over four months) left to return home, leaving some supplies buried at the base of a tree into which the message to dig had been carved. Burke dug up the supplies and put his own letter in the hole but foolishly covered it up before heading off again. A member of the relief group returned a few days later and presumed that the supplies had not been retrieved and the expedition had not returned. Burke and Wills both died as a result but King survived by living with Aborigines until found by a later rescue party.

There are several diferent types of desert landscapes in Australia. Almost two million square kilometres (about 38 percent of total desert area) is sand with the remainder divided fairly evenly between shield, stony, riverine/clay plains and upland/piedmont desert. Shield desert is the area where the ancient granite bedrock is the surface material. Shield desert regions are the Yilgarn Plateau (slightly north of a point midway between Perth and Kalgoorlie, WA) and the Arunta and Musgrave blocks within the ranges of central Australia.

Most of the remainder of the desert areas are also on the Western Shield but the shield is covered by other surface material. Stony desert is restricted to eastern lowlands where the silcrete caps (originally formed of various materials bonded together with silica about 30 million years ago) have been broken up into enormous plains of boulders and stones more commonly known as "gibbers". Riverine and clay pan deserts are floodplains and channels which rarely see any rain or contain flowing waters. Upland/piedmont deserts occur where old resistant rocks have been uplifted and stand as islands in sedimentary plains.

Ayers Rock is the world's largest monolith and the best recognised symbol of Australia's deserts. It is also one of Australia's most popular tourist attractions. From many kilometres away, the Rock rises as a solitary hump looming over the

Opposite: Holy Cross Toad (Notaden bennetti), Bourke, NSW.

Top: The Hammersley Range, WA.

Above: A Frillneck lizard (Chlamydosaurus kingi) erects its ruff-like frills to deter wouldbe attackers.

Opposite: An eagle sillouetted against the setting sun in the Pilbara,

Below: Chambers Pillar, a sandstone stack 45 metres high near the Finke River, NT is mainly remarkable by comparison with the surrounding featureless plains of central Australia. Named by John MacDouall Stuart (the first white man to see it) after James Chambers, an Adelaide backer of his expedition, Chambers Pillar is a remnant of an earlier mountain range which now only survives in the few places where a harder capping resisted the erosion which flattened the rest of the ranges.

featureless plains. It is 348 metres high and roughly square in plan with a diameter of about nine kilometres. The climb to the top over the smooth rock face with a rough texture is a feat of endurance under the hot desert sun. From the top, the desert stretches to infinity, the only visible natural feature of note the Olgas, 32 kilometres away.

Ayers Rock is made of a coarse hard sandstone which was formed underwater from eroded debris of high mountain ranges which existed 600 million years ago. Earth movements later tilted the remarkably uniform layers of sandstone almost vertically — the bands of Ayers Rock are at an angle of 75 degrees from their original horizontal position. About 110 million years ago. Ayers Rock was an island: caves around the base of the rock were created by wave action at this time. The surface of the Rock has been smoothed by the exfoliation of flakes of rock caused by the desert's extreme diurnal temperature differences.

Although Ernest Giles first sighted the rock from afar in 1872, it was not named until the following year when William Gosse examined and named it after Sir Henry Ayers, Premier of South Australia. Gosse waxed lyrical stating in his diary that "This rock is certainly the most wonderful natural feature I have ever seen". The name used by the local Pitjantjatjara Aborigines was "Uluru" — now the name of the National Park containing both Ayers Rock and the Olgas.

Whereas the underwater world of the Great Barrier Reef, Australia's other major tourist attraction, is a kaleidescope of colour, Ayers Rock is a vision of sombre tones. Even at sunset, the Rock takes on the hues of a glowing coal and during the day looks like an enormous piece of terra cotta sculpture. In comparison with the mountains — or even hills — of the east coast, Ayers Rock is not high. However, the impression of awesome grandeur created by Ayers Rock comes about because, when standing at its base, there is nothing to compare the Rock against — it stands alone as a solitary sentinel in a flat world.

Scenically, the Olgas are more attractive than Ayers Rock — their folds and

Opposite, top: A Pilbara anthill. Opposite, bottom: Mootwingee National Park near Broken Hill, NSW holds nearly all the remaining yellow-footed rock wallabies in the State.

Above, left:Water erosion has removed soil from around the roots of this River Red Gum (Eucalyptus camaldulensis) near the Flinders Ranges, SA.

Above, right: drought.

King's Canyon, NT.

Palm Valley, NT.

Outback landscape.

Sand dunes near Ayers rock.
Opposite: Mare's tail, high cirrus cloud, South Australia.

Opposite: lenticular (lens-shaped) clouds form when high altitude winds bounce over the lower air which has been pushed up in places by thermals.

Top: The Hammersley Range, WA.

Middle: The baobab tree (genus: Adansonia) is native only to northern Australia and tropical Africa.

Bottom: Kings Canyon, NT is home to numerous lizards.

Opposite: As if to emphasise the error of naming, the sun sets behind a tree on the Nullarbor ("no tree") Plain.

Above: the colours of central Australia — blue sky and the red sand of the Simpson Desert.

Top: bad erosion in NSW as arable land is washed away or swept away by wind.

Above: The salt lakes of inland Australia mark the end of many streams — instead of reaching the sea, they evaporate into the atmosphere leaving behind the salt they contained.

valleys hold the allure of the unknown and the arrangement of the domes like so many buns spilled from an oven provides endless photographic opportunities. But they have never captured the limelight as Ayers Rock has. Its brooding form remains in the mind of anyone who sees it — a looming presence at odds with, yet strangely reconciled to, the setting it dominates.

The Olgas take their name from the highest dome in the group — Mt Olga which is almost 890 metres above sea level and towers 546 metres above the surrounding plain. Ernest Giles also sighted it in 1872 and planned to name it in honour of his patron Baron von Mueller who instead persuaded him to name it after the Queen of Spain. The thirty domes and rocks in the Olgas group are made from a conglomerate — not the sandstone of Ayers Rock. They have weathered along vertical joint planes — producing steep sided ravines separating the monstrous cupolas of rock.

North of the Olgas, the Tanami track is a long lonely path from Alice Springs to Halls Creek, Western Australia. Near where it joins the Canning Stock Route there is one of the most remote — and remarkable — features of outback Australia: the Wolf Creek Meteorite Crater. Nine hundred and fourteen metres wide, the crater is the second largest of the world's positively identified meteorite craters: Coon Butte near Canyon Diablo in Arizona, USA is the largest — 1.6 kilometres wide. The meteorite which made the crater is estimated to have weighed as much as 50 000 tonnes.

In terms of the effect they have upon the earth, there are three categories of bodies which come on a collision course with this planet. Firstly, there are the harmless shooting stars — meteors which burn up in the atmosphere. Next there are those which are sufficiently large that they still retain some substantial mass after encountering the braking (and burning) effect of the earth's atmosphere.

These drop to the ground as meteorites — perhaps making an impression in the ground a few centimetres deep.

Finally there is the very occasional huge cosmic lump which is large enough to plough through the atmosphere without being stopped — or even slowed significantly — so it is still travelling at astronomical speeds (perhaps 100 000 kilometres per hour or more) when it hits the ground. The chunk of iron which threw up the crater at Wolf Creek was one of the big ones. Fortunately, this massive cosmic collision took place two million years ago. Since then, apart from almost filling the crater with sand, the desert environment has preserved the perfect symmetry of the Wolf Creek crater. Although kangaroo hunters had noticed the unusual landform since early this century, it was not till a geologist, Dr Frank Reeves, flew over it in 1947 and took some photos that it was brought to public attention and established to be a meteorite crater. The arid Australian climate is well suited to preserving meteorite craters: there are many others including ones at Henbury, NT and at Boxhole Station near Alice Springs.

The Kimberley region is also the area where the strange boab (or baobab) tree is found. It extends in an arc from the Kimberleys to Arnhemland and generally occurs within 150 kilometres of the coast. Although it doesn't grow very high, the boab tree can have a girth of 25 metres. Especially at night, boabs seem to take on a strangely humanoid appearance like distorted fat goblins dancing in the moving torchlight. Boab trees store large quantities of water in their trunks — Aborigines sometimes used them as water sources, sucking the moisture out through hollow reeds inserted into the trunk.

Although Australia is an ancient continent, attempts to tame the vast inland wilderness has only been undertaken in less than the two centuries of European settlement. Fortunately, the outback is vast enough to absorb these efforts with

Top: an aerial view of clouds forming over central Australia.

Above: Pebbles, released from conglomerate rocks by water erosion, cover the floor of this stream-bed in the Kimberley Ranges, WA.

Opposite: Palm Valley, NT.　　　　　*Top: A rock pool in Wearno Gorge, Hamersley Range, WA.*

little notable effect apart from a few roads across the desert plains. However, the mineral exploration boom of the last few decades and the advent of the recreational four-wheel drive vehicle is changing the pattern. Whereas a few years ago it was only necessary to camp a short distance away from formed roads to have the feeling of being alone in the expansive outback, these days you may have one or more vehicles drop in as they test their equipment or navigation away from defined tracks. The Easter break, for example, sees scores of four-wheel drives descending on the tiny community of Innamincka. I was there when one off-roader announced that he had found it necessary to winch himself out on the "dig" tree. It was reassuring to note that the whole pub fell into stunned silence.

As the outback desert is by definition uninhabitable, it should remain largely wilderness. To do this it may be necessary to introduce some general controls on vehicle use — perhaps limiting the use of off-road vehicles to defined tracks and restricting the number of destinationless tracks put in by mineral companies. But as any rules would be impossible to police, conservation will have to be left up to the good sense of the individual.

For over a hundred years, the outback deserts have been the forges upon which the unique Australian character has been cast. It's a harsh land with isolation forming a large part of its appeal. Dusty, hot and primitive — true wilderness — it isn't for everyone but those who like the subtle variations of desert landscapes will find an endless source of fascination.

A few years ago, I overheard a conversation in a Broken Hill caravan park washroom in which a distinctly English voice was declaring: "There are many attractions in Australia — it's unfortunate that there is so much space between them".

That space between is the real attraction of the Australian outback.

Middle: Mallee (low eucalpyts) and mulga (Acacia aneura) are two forms of vegetation which have lent their names to vast tracts of Australia.
Bottom: Ant colony, NT.

Index

Acknowledgements

The author wishes to thank the many people who have assisted and accompanied him in his journeys around Australia and gratefully acknowledges his use of information from the following books: Australia, a geography, D. N. Jeans (ed) (Sydney University Press); Presenting Australia's National Parks, Geoff Higgins, Leonard Cronin, Joanne McDonald (Child & Henry); Australia, A study of warm environments and their effect on British Settlement, Griffith Taylor (Methuen); Manual of Meteorology Parts 1 and 2, Australian Department of Science and Technology (AGPS); Australia's Natural Wonders, Michael Richardson (Golden Press); Australia the Beautiful Wilderness, Allan Moult (Weldons); Wild Australia (Readers Digest); Australia The Greatest Island, Robert Raymond (Ure Smith), Australian Museum Complete Book of Australian Mammals, Ronald Strahan (ed) (Angus & Robertson); What Bird Is That?, Neville W. Cayley (Angus & Robertson); National Parks of New South Wales, Graham Groves (Gregory's); Explore Australia, Lloyd O'Neil (Philip & O'Neil).

Photo-credits:

Robbi Newman's photographs appear on the following pages:

2, 6, 7, 8, 12(bottom three), 13, 14, 16, 17, 21, 22(ducks), 23, 24, 25, 26, 27, 29(Remarkable Cave), 30, 31, 32, 34, 36, 37, 39, 40(swan), 45(bottom three), 47(top), 53, 54(bottom), 55, 56, 57, 59, 60, 61, 72(middle), 76(top two), 77 (bottom right), 80, 81(bottom), 84, 90, 91, 93, 94, 95, 96, 97, 99, 100, 101, 102, 107, 109, 110, 111(bottom right), 113, 121, 122, 123, 124, 125, 126, 128, 130, 132, 133, 134, 135(bottom), 137, 142, 143, 144, 146, 149, 150, 151, 152, 153, 154 (top), 156, 157, back end papers.

Gunter Schmida's photographs appear on the following pages:
43(top), 52, 70, 71, 74, 75(top), 78, 81(top two), 82, 83, 85(two right), 135 (top two), 138, 139.

Thanks to Richard Bassett for the soaring photograph appearing at the bottom of   page 108 and Ed Ramsay for the plants photos on pages 87, 88, 89, 105, 140 and 141. All other photographs were taken by David McGonigal.